THE BIG BANG
Christmas Crackers
2000 – 2009

THE BIG BANG

Christmas Crackers
2000 – 2009

*being ten commonplace
selections by*

JOHN JULIUS NORWICH

THE DOVECOTE PRESS

First published in 2010 by The Dovecote Press Ltd
Stanbridge, Wimborne Minster, Dorset BH21 4JD

ISBN 978-1-904-34984-6
Introduction and this collection © John Julius Norwich 2010

Designed by The Dovecote Press
Typeset in 10/13 pt Sabon
Printed and bound by MPG Biddles Ltd, Kings Lynn, Norfolk

All papers used by The Dovecote Press are natural,
recyclable products made from wood grown in sustainable,
well-managed forests

A CIP catalogue record for this book is available
from the British Library

1 3 5 7 9 8 6 4 2

CONTENTS

'How these curiosities would be quite forgott, did not such idle fellowes as I putt them down.'

JOHN AUBREY

INTRODUCTION

I HAVE ALREADY WRITTEN INTRODUCTIONS to the three previous
volumes of this anthology. All were very much the same – the
Introductions, not I hope the volumes – and it is going to be pretty
hard to ring many changes on the fourth. (Owners of any of the first
three are excused from reading it anyway.) If on the other hand this
is the first time that you have encountered a collection of Christmas
Crackers, a few historical facts may not come amiss.

A little over half a century ago (I said they were historical) when I
was living in Beirut, my mother gave me a magnificent album, bound
in blue Nigerian goatskin, which she intended me to use as a visitors'
book. Alas, within a day or two of its arrival civil war broke out. A
curfew was declared and for several months we had no visitors at all.
Now it happened that for some years I had been noting down short
poems, paragraphs or miscellaneous items of one kind or another, that
had somehow caught my fancy and seemed worth remembering. There
were by now quite a few of them and the rather squalid little notebook
in which I had jotted them down was fast filling up. One evening that
still virgin album caught my eye, and I decided to copy them all in.

Suddenly I saw everything in an entirely different light. This
was no longer a heterogeneous pile of trivial jottings; it was my
commonplace book, a collection to be cultivated and treasured, on
which the exquisitely tooled and gilded leather seemed to confer a
wholly unexpected distinction. Some five years later, back in London,
the album was full and I ordered another, identical to the first except
that the goatskin was a rich burgundy red. This was followed in due
course by another, and another, with the colour changing each time.
At the time of writing – February 2010 – I have very nearly completed
the eleventh volume. (Scarlet, since you ask.)

I suppose it was inevitable that sooner or later I should fall victim to the come-up-and-see-my-etchings syndrome. Collections are no fun if they are not shared; and in the autumn of 1970 I decided to produce a little booklet containing a couple of dozen of my choicest items, and to send it round to a few friends as a sort of glorified Christmas card. Production costs, such as they were, might even be covered if I were to send a few extra copies to friendly booksellers, to dispose of them as best they could.

The edition disappeared with gratifying speed; still more gratifying was the reaction of a then unknown American lady – Alison Henning, who was subsequently to become a dear friend – who wrote to me asking for permission to print fifty more at her own expense. I replied that I should be delighted, on condition that she made it sixty and sent me ten. With this encouragement I risked another edition in 1971 – increasing my print order, in a burst of reckless optimism, from two hundred to three. That too sold out; and so it was that the uncertain seedling became a surprisingly hardy annual, and I now find myself introducing the combined harvest of its fourth decade. Of the ten most recent Crackers included here, only the front and back covers have been omitted. As before, however, there are certain additions, in the shape of a few afterthoughts of my own or of pertinent observations – and occasional corrections – from readers. These I have put in square brackets. I have also once again included as a bonus, at the end of each year's offering, a twenty-fifth entry which, being over a page in length, could not be included in an ordinary Cracker.

In the Introduction to the first bound volume (1970-79) I listed what seemed to me to be the advantages of a commonplace collection. 'First of all,' I pointed out, 'it costs literally nothing. Expensively-bound volumes are useful for providing the initial impetus and for creating the sense of pride that every collector must develop to keep him going, but they are in no way essential. Secondly it knows no restrictions of size or scope, being bound only by those limitations that the collector himself decides to impose; it follows that no other form of collection can so fully reflect his taste and personality. Thirdly, he is on his own, far away from the world of catalogues and sale-rooms. Indeed, one of the first lessons he learns is never to go out looking for anything; he is very unlikely to find it if he does, and the very act of searching seems in some way to blunt the antennae. He may not even need to wait until he next picks up a book; a chance remark, a letter from a friend, an opera programme, an advertisement, the instruction book for a new washing machine, a visit to a country church, a notice in a hotel room or railway station – any of these things, or a thousand others, can reveal the unexpected nugget of pure gold.'

But nowadays there is also another vital source. As the Crackers have gradually become better known, I now receive some superb contributions not only from old friends but from many people I have never met. This, admittedly, has one disadvantage: whereas in the early years virtually all the items I included were of my own finding, in recent years anything up to half the contents of any one Cracker may have come from elsewhere. Still, the consequent dent in my self-esteem is probably no bad thing, and is anyway negligible when compared with the pleasure at seeing the collection so magnificently enriched.

When these enrichments have appeared in a subsequent Cracker, I have always tried to give proper acknowledgement of their sources; but I am conscious of having occasionally failed to do so. When this lapse was due to a simple oversight, I have seized the present opportunity to repair it; but there have been, I fear, a number of occasions when, in my excitement at the gift, I somehow forgot to record the name of the giver. To any benefactors still unacknowledged I can only apologize, assuring them that my apparent ingratitude is due to sheer absent-mindedness, rather than to any desire to pass off their serendipity as my own.

To those who have sent me contributions that have not appeared, let me again emphasize that the annual Cracker is not, and never has been, composed of pieces collected during the previous twelve months. It is a selection made, normally in the course of a February weekend, from the entire corpus of the past half-century. One or two items may well have waited forty years or more before finally emerging in print. The mix is everything: the grave must lie down with the gay, the poetry with the prose, the cynical with the sad; and it is not always easy to make them do so. Moreover there remains plenty of marvellous material –

much of it of my own finding – which, though carefully transcribed into one of those eleven volumes, will never find its way into a Cracker. Sometimes it is simply unsuitable; more often than not I can offer no explanation, except to say that, just as novelists or playwrights frequently find their characters to be assuming personalities that were never intended or expected, so too the Crackers, in their modest way, seem to have developed an inner logic of their own. Some pieces fit; others refuse obstinately to settle down. I can only hope that their kind sponsors will understand, and not be discouraged from keeping up the good work.

For – as I said of its predecessor – this book is, I hope, only a milestone. It is not the end of the road. Soon after its publication the Cracker for 2010 will be on sale in all the usual bookshops – and I hope, indeed, a few more. Whether I shall be able to keep going for another ten years – by which time I shall be ninety – is anybody's guess; but – if only because I get more fun out of it all than anybody else does – I fully intend to go on till I drop.

To all those who have sent me contributions, used or unused, over the years I am equally and eternally grateful; and my very special thanks go to the Cracker's printers – formerly Livesey and Co of Shrewsbury, now Graphics & Print of Telford – who display endless patience over the proofs and nowadays design the jacket covers as well; finally to my secretary Marion Koenig, for the countless hours she spends on production, distribution and finance. Finally, my gratitude goes to all those, friends and strangers alike, who buy their Crackers year after year and have thus somehow managed to keep this whole slightly dotty show on the road for as long as they have.

John Julius Norwich

A
Christmas
Cracker

2000

A letter to the eight-year-old Charles Lutwidge Dodgson – future author of Alice in Wonderland, *from his father, the Rev. Charles Dodgson, Canon of Ripon Cathedral, written in January 1840.*

My dearest Charles,

I am very sorry that I had not time to answer your nice little note before. You cannot think how pleased I was to receive something in your handwriting, and you may depend on it I will not forget your commission. As soon as I get to Leeds I shall scream out in the middle of the street, *Ironmongers, Ironmongers.* Six hundred men will rush out of their shops in a moment – fly, fly, in all directions – ring the bell, call the constables, set the town on fire. I will have a file, a screwdriver and a ring and if they are not brought directly forth in forty seconds, I will leave nothing but one small cat alive in the whole town of Leeds, and I shall only leave that because I am afraid I shall not have time to kill it. Then what a bawling and tearing of hair there will be! Pigs and babies, camels and butterflies, rolling in the gutter together – old women rushing up the chimneys and cows after them – ducks hiding themselves in coffee-cups, and fat geese trying to squeeze themselves into pencil-cases. At last the Lord Mayor of Leeds will be found in a soup plate, covered up with custard and stuck full of almonds to make him look like a sponge cake that he may escape the dreadful destruction of the town. Oh! Where is his wife? She is safe in her own pincushion with a bit of sticking plaster on the top to hide the hump in her back, and all her dear children, seventy-eight poor little helpless infants crammed into her mouth, and hiding themselves behind her double teeth. Then comes a man hid in a teapot, crying and roaring, 'Oh, I have dropped my donkey. I put it up my nostril, and it has fallen out of the spout of the teapot into an old woman's thimble and she will squeeze it to death when she puts her thimble on.

At last they will bring the things which I ordered, and then I spare the town, and send off in fifty waggons, and under the protection of ten thousand soldiers, a file and a screwdriver and a ring as a present to Charles Lutwidge Dodgson from
his affectionate
Papa.

When James McNeill Whistler was forced by poverty to sell 'The White House' in Chelsea, he first placed an inscription above the front door. It ran:

Except the Lord build the house, they labour in vain that build it. E.W. Godwin, F.S.A., built this one.

Godwin, incidentally, lived for seven years with Ellen Terry – who was still technically married to G.F. Watts – and was the father by her of Gordon and Edith Craig. In 1875 he left her to marry Beatrix, the schoolgirl daughter of John Birnie Philip, sculptor of the frieze on the podium of the Albert Memorial. After his death, Beatrix married Whistler.

Baby, baby, naughty baby,
Hush, you squalling thing, I say,
Peace this moment, peace or maybe
Bonaparte will pass this way

Baby, baby, he's a giant,
Tall and black as Monmouth steeple,
And he breakfasts, dines and suppers
Every day on naughty people.

Baby, baby, if he hears you
As he gallops past the house,
Limb from limb at once he'll tear you,
Just as pussy tears a mouse.

And he'll beat you, beat you, beat you,
And he'll beat you all to pap,
And he'll eat you, eat you, eat you,
Every morsel, snap, snap, snap!

Nineteenth century English lullaby

15

From 'Sir Wilfred Grenfell: an Athletic Missionary', British Medical Journal, *19-26 December 1992:*

Grenfell was phenomenally fit. In middle life, after trudging 45 km. in one day with a backpack, he ran another eight to amputate a shattered leg, helped by two assistants, one of whom fainted. He proved the equal of the explorer Bob Bartlett on a hunting expedition, and enlarged an ice hole made for fishing to have a swim. Before they parted company he extracted Bartlett's tonsils, holding him against a shed wall.

In 1908 Grenfell nearly perished when he took his dog team, against advice, across Hare Bay in a short cut to an urgent case. The ice broke up and he drifted seawards on a floe. He had to kill three dogs and wrap himself in their skins to survive the night and then use their frozen legs to make a flag pole for waving his shirt. He was rescued by five oarsmen at great personal risk.

The next year, at the age of 44, on his way from Liverpool to New York on the *Mauretania,* he proposed to a girl 20 years younger, after a three-day acquaintance. On being reminded that he did not even know her name, he replied that he was only interested in what it was going to be . . .

His selfless sincerity and irrepressible sense of humour won him unyielding affection, but his application of the principle 'start something, someone else will finish it' could make him an exasperating colleague . . .

Humphrey Burton has drawn my attention to the Schultz-Lorentzen Dictionary of the West Greenland Eskimo Language, *published in 1927. Here are four short entries:*

Ata, sulôrsimavutit!

Well, now you have again relieved yourself in your trousers!

Nivgornêrqutigssag

Something to take away the taste of fish.

Orssùnguvoq

To feel sick from having eaten too much blubber.

Pugtârpoq

To leap from one iceberg to another.

The life of this Clerk was just threescore and ten
Nearly half of which time he had sung out Amen.
In his youth he was married like other young men,
But his wife died one day so he chaunted Amen:
A second he took, she departed, what then?
He married and buried a third with Amen.
Thus his joys and his sorrows were Treble, but then
His voice was deep Bass as he sung out Amen,
On the Horn he could blow just as well as most men,
So his Horn was exalted in blowing Amen.
But he lost all his wind after threescore and ten,
And here with three wives he waits till again
The Trumpet shall rouse him to sing out Amen.

Epitaph in the churchyard of
Crayford, Kent, to Peter Isnell,
Clerk of the Parish, d.1811

PARIS, June 5 (AP) – France's synchronized swim team had its Olympics program worked out: in black bathing suits, they would goose-step in German military style to the side of the pool.

Then, diving in, they would re-enact the arrival of Jewish women in the death camps, selection by Nazi doctors and their march to the gas chambers.

While the team's leader defended the program as art, Sports Minister Guy Drut decided it might offend crowds in Atlanta. He ordered a change.

The team had planned to perform the four-minute program, set to music from Steven Spielberg's *Schindler's List* and to chants sung in Jewish ghettos before the holocaust . . .

The French sports daily *L'Equipe* condemned the team for using one of history's darkest periods as an entertainment theme. The team's technical director, Jean-Paul Clemençon, defended the program, saying it had 'great emotional value'.

Newsday, June 6 1996

Long ago, in the 1987 Cracker, *I transcribed a superb pastiche of Milton by Sir Edward Marsh. My pen-friend Mr Carraigh Thompson of Patmos has recently drawn my attention to another from the same source, to be found in the 1946 volume of* New Statesman Competitions:

MILTON AND GASTRONOMY

(Since Milton's day the art of cookery has made great progress. This passage of twenty lines should be interpolated in the account of the banquet in Book II of *Paradise Regained.*)

[All fish from sea or shore . . . for which was drain'd
Pontus, and Lucrine bay, and *Afric* coast.]

Nor wanted those that to a later time
Yielded their subtil flavours, *Natives* light
Of *Colchester,* and Trout cerulean[1],
Sole-mornay, or Langusta; and a Sauce
Imagin'd rather oft than elsewhere found
By *Escofier, Bulestin* or *Vatel*
With delicatest inspiration: Soups
Mulligatawny, Bisk, Minestra, Borch,
These clear, they thick, *Lucullan* Fables true,
If true, here only, and with concomitant
Toast which th' Australian Nightingale resounds[2],
Not th' *Attic,* season'd well with lively Salt
Of *Cerebos* and whitest noonday born.
For Meat, that toothsome Pasty, quaintly call'd'
Of Business-woman on the breeze a-wing[3],
And Ducks of Rouen prest, with Cherries round
Redning[4], and hares ineffably injugged:
Fruits costly enow to satisfy the Spouse
Of *Tanqueray*[5], Pineapple, Prickly Pear

A CHRISTMAS CRACKER – 2000

Of Avocado, Mango, or Mangosteen.
[Alas, how simple, to these cates compar'd,
Was that crude apple that diverted Eve.]

[1]*Truite au bleu.*
[2]Toast Melba.
[3]*Vol-au-vent à la financiére.*
[4]*Canard de Rouen à la Montmorency.*
 [5]'I do like fruit, when it's expensive.'

John Milton died on 8 November 1674 and was buried at the London church of St Giles without Cripplegate. In 1793 his grave was opened; the story is told in the superb London Encyclopaedia, *edited by Ben Weinreb and Christopher Hibbert:*

A journeyman named Holmes procured a mallet and chisel . . . forcing open the coffin so that the corpse (which was clothed in a shroud, and looked as if it had only just been buried) might be seen. Mr Fountain, one of the overseers, then endeavoured to pull out the teeth but, being unsuccessful, a bystander took up a stone and loosened them with a blow. There were only five in the upper jaw, but they were quite white and good. They, together with some of the lower ones, Mr Fountain [and two other men] divided between them. A rib bone was also taken and the hair from the head, which was long and smooth and torn out by the handful. After this the caretaker Elizabeth Grant took the coffin under her care, charging sixpence to anyone who wished to view it. Later she reduced her fee to threepence and finally to twopence.

From the transcript of a court case in Boston, Massachusetts:

Attorney: Did you check the body for signs of life?
Pathologist: No.
Attorney: Did you check to see whether the body was breathing or not?
Pathologist: I did not.
Attorney: Did you check the pulse?
Pathologist: I did not.
Attorney: So how could you be sure that the patient was in fact dead?
Pathologist: Because his brain was in a jar on my desk.
Attorney: But he could, possibly, have been alive?
Pathologist: And probably practising law in Massachusetts.

Crown'd with flowers I saw fair Amaryllis
   By Thyrsis sit, hard by a fount of Chrystal,
And with her hand more white than snow or lilies,
   On sand she wrote, *My faith shall be immortal:*
And suddenly a storm of wind and weather
   Blew all her faith and sand away together.

Anon., 1611

Ernest Block died in Portland, Oregon, in 1959. He was Swiss by birth and American by adoption; but above all he was Jewish, and although he wrote much in a purely western idiom (including an opera of Macbeth) *it is for his 'Jewish' music –* Schelomo, Avodath Hakodesh, Scenes from Jewish Life, *etc. – that he is best known. He explained it like this:*

It is not my purpose, nor my desire, to attempt a 'reconstruction' of Jewish music, or to base my works on melodies that are more or less authentic. I am not an archaeologist. I hold it of first importance to write good, genuine music, my music. It is the Jewish soul that interests me, the complex, glowing, agitated soul, that I feel vibrating throughout the Bible; the freshness and naïveté of the Patriarchs; the violence that is evident in the prophetic books; the Jews' savage love of justice; the despair of the Preacher in Jerusalem; the sorrow and immensity of the Book of Job; the sensuality of the Song of Songs. All this is in us, and it is the better part of me. All that I endeavour is to hear in myself, and to transcribe in my music, the venerable emotion of the race that slumbers way down in my soul.

On 16 December 1893 – when Parliament had been in continuous session for eleven months and it had been announced that members would have only four days' recess at Christmas – Mr Gladstone received a letter in a neat but childish hand, written on ruled paper, from the infant son of the Earl of Pembroke:

Dear Mr Gladstone,

I am sorry we cannot go to Ireland for Christmas, as you have only given Father four days holiday. And I hope you will give him some more after this letter.

Yours sincerely,

George Sidney Herbert

Gladstone replied the same day:

My dear Boy,

It is very sad. I feel for you. And I feel with you. As you cannot get to Ireland, so I cannot get home, at Christmas. And you, I hope, will have many, very many, very happy Christmasses. But I, having had eighty-three already, feel that I am taking one of my last chances.

Can anything be done? Not by me. But I think your Father could do something, if he thought it right to ask some ten or a dozen of his friends to abate a little the number and length of their speeches. For they are so fond of him that I believe they would do it. But I could not expect them to do it for my asking. If they did it for him, there is no saying whether it might enable you to go to Ireland.

With best wishes for Christmas, Easter, and all other times,

Ever yours,

W. E. Gladstone

On 8 January 1687 at the church of the Feuillants in Paris, France's greatest composer, Jean-Baptiste Lully, conducted more than a hundred and fifty musicians in a performance of his Te Deum, *celebrating the recovery of King Louis XIV from an operation. In those days conductors used a long staff, rather than the modern baton, to beat time; and Lully, in the excitement generated by one particularly emotional passage, brought this staff forcibly down on his own toe. An abscess developed; gangrene set in; and on the morning of 22 March he died.*

Despite an apparently affectionate wife and six children – of whom the three sons all became composers – Lully's natural proclivities lay all too obviously in other directions; on at least one occasion he received a royal reprimand. So it was that after his death the Sieur de Saint-Evremond – one of the few Frenchmen, incidentally, to have been buried in Westminster Abbey – wrote the following little verse:

D'Orphée et de Lully le mérite est semblable;
Je trouve cependant de la diversité
Sur un certain sujet assez considérable:
Si Lully quelque jour descendait aux Enfers
Avec un plein pouvoir de grâces et de peines,
Un jeune criminel sortirait de ses fers –
Une pauvre Eurydice y garderait ses chaines.

Which could be very freely translated:

Orpheus and Lully had some qualities to share;
The fact remains, however – as we're all too well aware –
That in one respect they differed as a circle from a square:
If Lully had gone down to Hell, of special powers possessed
To set free those he fancied and to punish all the rest,
The bonds of some young rascal he would eagerly dissever –
While poor forlorn Eurydice remained in chains for ever.

My friend David Langford has produced a marvellous piece by Augustus Hare:

I recall visiting the late Dean of Christ Church, known as Presence-of-Mind Smith. 'In my life', he said, 'there has been one most fortunate incident. A friend of mine persuaded me to go out with him in a boat upon a lake. I did not wish to go, but he persuaded me and I went. By the intervention of Providence I took my umbrella with me. We had not been long on the lake when the violence of the waves threw my friend out of the boat drowning, and he sank. Soon, as is the case with drowning persons, he came up again, and clutched hold of the side of the boat. Then, such providentially was *the presence of my mind*, that I seized my umbrella and rapped him violently on the knuckles till he let go. He sank and I was saved.'

In The Story of My Life *Hare tells of his youth in the 1840s – he was actually born in 1834 – when his family was living at Stoke, near Market Drayton in Shropshire, and travelled frequently between there and London:*

Long after the railway was made we continued to go in our own carriage, posting, to Shropshire. Gradually my mother consented to go in her own carriage, on a truck, by rail as far as Birmingham; farther she could not endure it. Later still, nearly the whole journey was effected by rail, but in our own chariot. At last we came to use the ordinary railway carriages, but then, for a long time, we used to have post-horses to meet us at some station near London; my mother would not be known to enter London in a railway carriage – 'it was so excessively improper' (the sitting opposite strangers in the same carriage); so we entered the metropolis 'by hand', as it was called in those early days of railway travelling.

As I compile this Cracker, a heroic handful of British tradesmen is fighting a rearguard action against the determination of the European Union to force the metric system upon them. They would have enjoyed the enthusiastic support of Lord Palmerston, who wrote in 1860:

Can you expect that the people of the United Kingdom will cast aside all the names of space and weight and capacity which they learnt from their infancy and all of a sudden adopt an unmeaning jargon of barbarous words representing Ideas and Things new to their minds? It seems to me to be a dream of pedantic Theorists . . .

I see no use however in attempting to Frenchify the English nation, and you may be quite sure that the English nation will not consent to be Frenchified.

Licensed Victuallers'
Home for the Aged
Bevendean Road
Brighton, Sussex

19 December 1974

Dear John,

I want to thank you for your lovely gift of a table radio. It is wonderful that an absolute stranger as yourself to remember people like us.

I am 82 years of age, and has been in the home for 16 years. They treat us very well but the loneliness is sometimes very hard to bear. My room mate Mrs Ernstadt who is a very nice person, but she is very selfish. She has a table radio, but she will not let me use it, she turns it off when I come into the room, now I have one of my own.

My son and daughter in law are very nice and they come & visit me once a month. I appreciate it, but I know they come out of a sense of duty & obligation. This is why your gift is all the more welcome, because it was given, not from a sense of duty, but more a feeling of compassion for a fellow human-being.

Today Mrs Ernstadt's radio went out of order & she asked me whether she could listen to mine. I told her to go and fuck herself.

Yours sincerely,
Mrs Greenfield.

I have seen a photocopy of this letter and am virtually certain that it is genuine.

Past Crackers have included one or two inspired parodies by Sir Laurence Jones – who, as 'L.E.J.', was an almost weekly winner of the New Statesman *Weekend Competitions half a century ago. Here is an original poem of his:*

Lines to a Bishop who was shocked (A.D. 1950) at seeing a
Pier-glass in a Bathroom

Beneath that Chasuble, my Lord, that holds
You close (as Charity all men enfolds)
Beneath that Cope that, opening before,
Of Life Eternal signifies the Door,
And (as Durandus taught) recalls the strength
Of godly Perseverance by its length;
Beneath that Rocket of pure lawn, and whiter
Than Iceland's winter cap; beneath that Mitre,
A body stands concealed, which God once chose
The Spirits of his Children to enclose,
And (as a Bishop surely must believe)
His Very Self Incarnate to receive.
Yet, through a mirror suddenly aware
That 'Temples of the Spirit' can be bare,
You shrink aghast, with pained and puzzled eyes,
While God's great laughter peals about the skies.

Music is a form of human expression that on the page is dead. It lives when the first note is sounded and it dies as the final note dies away. After that comes the applause: beautiful but dangerous. I always say, we must not bring the applause home with us; we must leave it there. If it means anything it is not 'Bravo!' but 'Thank You'. My eldest son is a surgeon. He saves life, but he receives no applause. Applause is for the footballer, for the acrobat in the circus. It would be inhuman not to enjoy it. But, please, leave it there. Afterwards, all we can ask is: 'How, next time, can we do it better?'

Carlo Maria Giulini

William Hone was a publisher, bookseller and political satirist – and a lifelong friend of George Cruikshank, who illustrated many of his books and pamphlets. He was, however, hopeless with money – a failing which led to his being more than once arrested for debt – and generally quite unable to cope with life around him. This letter to Cruikshank reveals his character as well as anything could:

45 Ludgate Hill

17 November 1825

Dear George,

You cannot come on Sunday – *there's* a *go*! I have received orders 'not to sleep out at night any more; until' & 'not to stay out late', nor to be 'out of the way' – in short I am to be 'within call', I may be 'wanted', it's not known 'how soon', – and I'm 'very foolish' – and I'm 'quite ridiculous', – and all this I'm told to my head – and I feel myself so. From present appearances I think it likely that my daughter's son may have an uncle or aunt born, on or about, or before or after, or near unto Sunday next, and now, ensuing – so 'you *see*'!

Now will you tell this to Mrs C. – and tell her she was 'right', & I was 'wrong' – and say I am much obliged to her – for although I have asked the 'old Lady' 'when?' and 'what time?' & so forth I have never got out more than 'soon' – and 'it's all time enough' – and on pressing the matter further, have had 'phi!', 'stuff', 'fiddle', 'how inquisitive you are', and 'how can *I* tell?', and all and every such sort of answers, till now, that on telling her you and Mrs C. – were coming on Sunday, '*off* she goes' and tells me *plump,* that I 'ought to have known better', (though *she* has kept *me* in ignorance) and that if I 'had not been a *goose*' I should not have done it – whereupon I rejoin that *she* was the 'goose', and I was the 'gander', 'or I should *not* have done it' – and this upon she says '*that's* the way I *always* do things!' Oh dear!

I perceive, *now,* how to manage her 'the *next*-time'! and so

33

I tell her, and she huffs, – and I get nothing but snubs, and she asks me what I 'can say to Mr and Mrs Cruikshank'?, and tells me how I shall 'look', and all that. If you don't choose to come and see how I 'look' (and I advise you not) just imagine it, and tell me how you *think* I look.

> I am, dear George,
> My wife's – oh dear!
> W. Hone.

He had twelve children altogether.

From Jane and Michael Thomas come these two little gems by Godfrey Turton:

AT THE THEATRE: A TRIOLET AND A RONDEL

Triolet (on a cue taken by an actress playing a small part):

> 'Im wunderschönen Monat Mai,'
>   sang Harlequin to Columbine,
>   and the packed house was thrilled; but I –
>   O *wunderschöner Monat Mai* –
>   watched you come unobtrusively
>   and join them midway through the line;
>   'Im *wunderschönen Monat Mai*'
>   sang Harlequin to Columbine.

Rondel (on the occupant of a seat a few rows in front in the stalls):

> Feeling her beauty flow into my mind
> and sweetly flood the channels of my brain,
> till all cognition foundered in inane
> and blissful adoration undefined,
> I watched the short curls melt, honey combined
> with milk, on her bare neck, a golden stain,
> feeling her beauty flow into my mind
> and sweetly flood the channels of my brain.
> Was it then necessary, sir, or kind
> that you with your enormous head should crane
> across the view I thirsted to retain
> (although I only saw her from behind)
> feeling her beauty flow into my mind?

In the 1992 Cracker *I quoted a Chicago newspaper reporting the Gettysburg Address. Here are one or two other critical misjudgements. First, by the* Quarterly Review *in 1848, on* Jane Eyre:

Jane Eyre is throughout the personification of an unregenerate and undisciplined spirit . . . It pleased God to make her an orphan, friendless and penniless – yet she thanks nobody, and least of all Him, for the food and raiment, the friends, companions and instructors of her helpless youth. On the contrary, she looks on all that has been done for her not only as her undoubted right, but as falling far short of it . . .

Altogether the autobiography of Jane Eyre is pre-eminently an anti-Christian composition. There is throughout it a murmuring against the comforts of the rich and against the privations of the poor, which is a murmuring of God's appointment – there is a proud and perpetual assertion of the rights of man, for which we find no authority in God's Word or in God's providence . . . We do not hesitate to say that the tone of mind and thought which has overthrown and violated every code human and divine abroad, and fostered Chartism and rebellion at home, is the same which has also written *Jane Eyre*.

And how about Lord Byron:

Why don't they review and praise *Solomon's Guide to Health?* It is better sense and as much poetry as Johnny Keats.

The Athenaeum *on* Das Rheingold:

Never was there such a storm in a slop-basin.

And Tchaikovsky on a rival:

I played over the music of that scoundrel Brahms. What a giftless bastard! It annoys me that this self-inflated mediocrity is hailed as a genius. Why, in comparison with him, Raff is a giant, not to speak of Rubinstein, who after all is a live and important human being, while Brahms is chaotic and absolutely empty and dried-up stuff.

Finally, Columbia Studios after the first audition of Marilyn Monroe:

Can't act . . . Voice like a tight squeak . . . utterly unsure of herself . . . Unable even to take refuge in her own insignificance.

And on Fred Astaire:

Can't act. Slightly bald. Also dances.

As *everybody must know by now, the year 2000 was the centenary of the death of John Ruskin. Here is the last paragraph* of Praeterita, *his last book; and these are consequently the last sentences he ever wrote for publication:*

Fonte Branda I last saw with Charles Norton, under the same arches where Dante saw it. We drank of it together, and walked together that evening on the hills above, where the fireflies among the scented thickets shone fitfully in the still undarkened air. *How* they shone! moving like fine-broken starlight through the purple leaves. How they shone! through the sunset that faded into thunderous night as I entered Siena three days before, the white edges of the mountainous clouds still lighted from the west, and the openly golden sky calm behind the Gate of Siena's heart, with its still golden words, *Cor magis tibi Sena pandit,* and the fireflies everywhere in the sky and cloud rising and falling, mixed with the lightning, and more intense than the stars.

To the strand of the daughters of the sunset,
The apple-tree, the singing and the gold . . .

Hippolytus
Tr. Gilbert Murray

BONUS

Hilaire Belloc was a great friend of my parents. I well remember this burly black-clad figure in his wing-collar and cloak arriving at our holiday home in Sussex for lunch, and the old French songs that he used to sing in his cracked old voice. For me he is the greatest comic poet in the English language; but his serious verse is, at its best, well worth remembering. His Heroic Poem in Praise of Wine – which, incidentally, he dedicated to my father – is much too long; what follows is considerably abridged:

To exalt, enthrone, establish and defend,
To welcome home mankind's mysterious friend
Wine, true begetter of all arts that be;
Wine, privilege of the completely free;
Wine the recorder, wine the sagely strong;
Wine, bright avenger of sly-dealing wrong,
Awake, Ausonian Muse, and sing the vineyard song!

But what are these, that from the outer murk
Of dense mephitic vapours creeping lurk
To breathe foul airs from that corrupted well
Which oozes slime along the floor of Hell?
These are the stricken palsied brood of sin
In whose vile veins, poor, poisonous and thin,
Decoctions of embittered hatreds crawl;
These are the Water-Drinkers, cursed all!
On what gin-sodden Hags, what flaccid sires
Bred these White Slugs from what exhaust desires?
In what close prison's horror were their wiles
Watched by what tyrant power with evil smiles;
Or in what caverns, blocked from grace and air,
Received they, then, the mandates of despair?

For such as these in vain the Rhine has rolled
Imperial centuries by hills of gold;
For such as these the flashing Rhone shall rage
in vain its lightning through the Hermitage
Or level-browed divine Touraine receive
The tribute of her vintages at eve.
For such as these Burgundian heats in vain
Swell the rich slope or load the empurpled plain.
Bootless for such as these the mighty task
Of bottling God the Father in a flask
And leading all Creation down distilled
To one small ardent sphere immensely filled.
With memories empty, with experience null,
With vapid eyeballs meaningless and dull
They pass unblest through the unfruitful light;
And when we open the bronze doors of Night,
When we in high carousal, we reclined,
Spur up to Heaven the still ascending mind,
Pass with the all-inspiring, to and fro,
The torch of genius and the Muse's glow,
They, lifeless, stare at vacancy alone
Or plan mean traffic, or repeat their moan.
We, when repose demands us, welcomed are
In young white arms, like our great Exemplar
Who, wearied with creation, takes his rest
And sinks to sleep on Ariadne's breast.
They through the darkness into darkness press,
Despised, abandoned and companionless.
And when the course of either's sleep has run,
We leap to life like heralds of the sun;
We from the couch in roseate mornings gay
Salute as equals the exultant day
While they, the unworthy, unrewarded they,
The dank despisers of the Vine, arise
To watch grey dawns and mourn indifferent skies.

. . . So, my friend,
Let not Your cup desert me in the end.
But when the hour of mine adventure's near
Just and benignant, let my youth appear
Bearing a Chalice, open, golden, wide,
With benediction graven on its side.
So touch my dying lip: so bridge that deep:
So pledge my waking from the gift of sleep,
And, sacramental, raise me the Divine
Strong brother in God and last companion, Wine.

A Christmas Cracker

2001

From The Week, *8 January 2000:*

The land-locked country Swaziland has lost its entire merchant navy. The fleet, which consists of just one ship, has disappeared. But Transport Minister Ephraem Magagula is not worried. 'The situation is absolutely under control. We believe it is in the sea somewhere,' he told the *Johannesburg Star.* 'At one time we sent a team of men to look for it, but there was a problem with drink and they failed to find it. But I categorically reject all suggestions of incompetence on the part of this government. The *Swazimar* is a big ship painted in the sort of nice bright colours you can see at night. Mark my words, it will turn up.'

As all too many of us know all too well, the world is full of people who appear to have nothing better to do than to write sublimely dotty letters to other people whom they have never met. The marvellous Hermione, Lady Ranfurly, who died early this year, was moved some years ago to write a sort of compendium reply to them all. (At least I assume that that is what it is.)

Great Pednor
Chesham
Buckinghamshire
HP5 2SU

15 September 1994

Dear Mrs Sickmuller,

I have your kind letter about my book *and* your book and am grateful for your praise, and tips on food, sex and plumbing.

I am amazed, and so sorry, about your family tragedies and specially horrified about your grandson drowning in your earthen closet when playing Hide and Seek.

Yes, I love animals but have, so far, never kept a boa constrictor. Yours sounds adorable.

I will try to write to your cousins, your aunt and your vicar when next I have a moment. No, I don't wear a wig tho' I am over 80. So far I have my own teeth and 1½ bosoms. So good of you to advise me about facial hair, warts and body odour. This will be a huge help to me.

Wonderfully kind of you to write so fully to me, and your tips will be a godsend, particularly those about sex in old age, the dangers of armpits and big toes, and lice.

I shall treasure your letter as long as I live.

Best wishes to you, your 13 children and your boa. Also messages to your 4th husband. It was kind and generous of you to write as you did and to send me such good advice.

Yours sincerely,
Hermìone Ranfurly

This was my first time to see *Fidelio*. Arnold and Margaret had seen it in Lisbon, the very night the Salazar dictatorship ended: the soldiers in the plot of the opera, when they had come on to the stage that night, had had red carnations in the barrels of their guns, like the real soldiers of the 'bloodless revolution' out on the streets. In the first act there is a quartet, *Mir ist so wunderbar*. The four protagonists come down to the footlights, and they do that thing that happens in opera — seemingly unknown to each other, they each sing their line of music out straight to the audience, as if it is not of their doing that the lines intermingle in a complex and perfect harmony that it takes the four of them to make, but that it is a separate thing from each of them. I was transfixed, as I always am by ensemble singing. When the curtain came down on the act I wiped the tears from my eyes and I said to Arnold: 'Why is ensemble singing so beautiful? What makes it move us so much?' And he said: 'People would be like that all the time, if they could.'

Nuala O'Faolain
Are You Somebody?

This bird was happy once in the high trees.
You cage it in your cellar, bring it seed,
Honey to sip, all that its heart can need
Or human love can think of: till it sees,
Leaping too high within its narrow room,
The old familiar shadow of the leaves,
And spurns the seed with tiny, desperate claws.
Nought but the woods despairing pleads,
The woods, the woods again, it grieves, it grieves.

Boethius
(Tr. Helen Waddell)

Nancy Lindsay was an ill-kempt and eccentric figure who was a distant cousin of mine. She grew shrub-roses in Sutton Courtenay, near Abingdon. Here are a few extracts from her catalogue.

ALBA: 'Amelia'. An elegy from the battlefield of Minden, near on two centuries ago, the lovely mist-green foliage and silken rose-madder petals still grace the ancient owl-grey stones of Winchester's cathedral precincts.

'Rose de Resht'. Happened on it in an old Persian garden in ancient Resht. Tribute of the tea caravans plodding Persia-wards from China over the Central Asian steppes, it is a sturdy yard-high bush of glazed lizard-green, perpetually emblazoned with full camelia flowers of pigeon's-blood ruby irised with royal-purple, haloed with dragon-sepals like the painted blooms on oriental faience.

BOURBONIANA: 'General Oudinot'. Great cabbages of bloodie crimson lustred with a sable sheen.

GALLICA: 'Duchesse de Buccleuch'. Rollicking bushes with flaunting leaves of arrogant Sevres-green; the massive razed, ruched, quartered blooms are of a rich, ripe strawberry.

HYBRID PERPETUAL: 'Due de Cazes'. A bold bush with patrician foliage of burnished bottle-green. The full petalled chalices glow with vintage purple of sultry burgundy.

'Witch's Caprice'. Buxom, gofered extravaganzas of strawberry-rose, candy-striped fuchsia, like porcelain cabbages fashioned by a witty potter.

MIRIFICA: 'Sacramento Rose'. The 'Gooseberry Rose' is found only in the Sacramento Mountains of New Mexico out of all the world, spreading into little thickets of graceful, goldenprickled, celadon-green stems set with tiny grape-green fretted leaves, spangled with lovely flowers of shimmering Tyrrhian-pink with centres of yellow silk. The spur glass buds are chrysoprase and the hips of amber and apricot match the so sweet goosegogs of our childhood.

MOYESII: 'La Giralda', 'Nevada'. Averred to be the offspring of the fee-fo-fum Chinese briar and the graceful, delicate Spanish tea-rose, the glorious 'Nevada' owns to little of its parentage, reputed, in its deportment, being a great, shining jade shrub bowed-down under the opulence of its delectable tasty moon-flowers, waxing pearly-white and waning a dawn-pink.

MUSCOSA: 'Deuille [sic] de Paul Fontaine'. This celebrated rare and curious Phoenix, barbed as the porcupine, displays grandiose cabbages of sombre-glowing black ruby, empurpled ebony and plutonic copper.

OMIENSIS: 'Hidcote Gold'. Brought from Yunnan by Major Lawrence Johnson in the 1930s, a gigantic briar with awesome ruddy-thorned canes and feathery fern-leaves of parrot-green; in blossom a coruscating cataract of sequins of candied gilt, in autunm a-twinkle with a myriad coral-scarlet beads.

SPINOSISSIMA: 'William IV'. A very distinct dwarf, suckering hither and thither but sadly slow-growing

(A daffodil named after my mother was once advertised in a catalogue – not Nancy's – as 'The Lady Diana Manners: good for all purpose'. She always maintained that it was the best compliment she ever received.)

Here is a letter from George Sand to her lover Alfred de Musset, dated 18 October 1845. The full purport of it becomes clear only when one reads the alternate lines:

Très cher ami,

> Je suis émue de vous dire que j'ai
> bien compris l'autre jour que vous aviez
> toujours une folle envie de me faire
> danser. Je garde un souvenir de votre
> baiser et je voudrais que ce soit
> une preuve que je puisse être aimée
> par vous. Je suis prête à vous montrer mon
> affection toute désintéressée et sans cal-
> cul car si vous voulez me voir aussi
> vous dévoiler sans artifice mon âme
> toute nue, daignez me rendre visite,
> nous causerons entre amis. Franchement
> je montrerai que je suis une femme
> sérieuse, capable de vous offrir l'affection
> la plus profonde comme la plus étroite
> amitié, en un mot, la meilleure épouse
> que vous puissiez imaginer. Puisque votre
> âme est triste, pensez que la solitude su-
> bite est longue, bien dure et souvent
> pénible. Aussi en échange, l'âme é-
> branlée, accourez done bien vite me la
> faire oublier. A l'amour, je veux me sou-
> mettre entièrement.

George Sand

Book beginnings: among the worst, I should certainly include the opening sentence of The Last Days of Pompeii, *by Edward Bulwer-Lytton:*

> 'Ho, Diomed, well met! Do you sup with Glaucus tonight?' said a young man of small stature, who wore his tunic in those loose and effeminate folds which proved him to be a gentleman and a coxcomb.

Among the best, how about that of Earthly Powers, *by Anthony Burgess?*

> It was in the afternoon of my eighty-first birthday, and I was in bed with my catamite when Ali announced that the Archbishop had come to see me.

I had somehow always assumed this last to be by Ronald Firbank – he who, when asked by a friend what to order in a Lyons Corner House, said:

> Ask for heron's eggs, whipped with wine into an amber foam.

In December 1962 President Kennedy and Prime Minister Harold Macmillan met in Nassau. My friend Brian Porter has sent me the following short scene he wrote after the Conference. He tells me that he believes it to be quite a fair approximation to what actually occurred.

A British reporter waylays the Prime Minister as he enters the building.

Reporter: Prime Minister, what do you hope to get out of this?

Macmillan (barely audibly): Polaris.

Inside the Conference Room, the Americans sit down one side of the table, the British down the other. The President and the Prime Minister face each other in the middle.

JFK: Well, gentlemen, the British have made an official request for Polaris. Should we accede to this request?

George Ball: Mr President, I protest. We should not discuss this in the presence of the British. No, sir!

JFK: Well, we're all in this together. It may be in America's interest.

GB: Mr President, we should discuss this in private. It's an American matter. Hell, sir, we'd be dumb . . .

Mac: Jack, *(indicating Ball)* who is that?

JFK: That's George Ball.

Mac (ruminatively): What a singular name . . .

JFK: Well, Prime Minister, would you like to put your case?

Mac: Ah, yes. You see. When I was a young man. Up at Oxford.

I had many friends there. All in the flower of their youth. It was a golden summer. There was the glint of sculls on the water. There was the sound of bat upon ball. And the merry laughter of girls . . . And then that terrible day. Someone had shot the Archduke and things were never the same again . . . Within a year . . . most of my friends had gone . . . cut down like wheat before the scythe . . .

(Dead silence, broken only by an occasional American sob)

. . . And back home. The unbearable heartache . . . the empty stirrup. The faithful old pointer awaiting his master's call – the call that would never come again . . . And those once carefree girls . . . the pallor on their brows . . . the dreaded telegram. How sad it was, you know . . . how very sad . . .

(There is not a dry eye in the room: the Americans tearful with emotion, the British with the effort of trying to keep a straight face.)

JFK (gulping): Has . . . the Prime Minister . . . satisfied you?

(They nod, weakly. The meeting breaks up. The Prime Minister, looking about 100 and very bent, walks slowly to the door. The Americans make way for him.)

Mac (to the reporter outside the building, very softly): I think we've got it.

My friend Roy Dean sends me this gem:

Heartcry from Troy

Move up a little, Menelaus, please;
The sharp end of your spear
Is sticking in my ear,
And I am very ill at ease.

Your elbow, Neoptolamus, is hard;
Remove it from my eye
Or later we shall try
Our skill at arms with nothing barred.

Who thought of this contraption anyhow?
Athene? Yes, she would!
I'd like to know what good
We're doing sitting in this cow.

Perhaps it *is* a horse; I do not care
To argue in this heat.
Here you! Get off my feet!
Hold off, Diomedes – give me air.

O fool device! O idiot resource!
A hundred locked in here.
Stay off, I'm feeling queer!
Is there a doctor in the horse?

R.G.G. Price

(Strangely enough, in the last line of the fourth verse the original name given was 'Horatio', which is not remotely Greek. I have taken the liberty of changing it to 'Diomedes'; I hope the author will forgive me.)

I never tire of stories about Tennyson; past Crackers have been full of them. Geoffrey Madan notes that in the poet's copy of Paradise Lost, *opposite the line (V,336)*

Taste after taste upheld with kindliest change

he had written two words in the margin: 'French cook'.

From G.M. Young's Romanes Lecture on Gladstone, I learn that

'of Tennyson Jowett once observed, mysteriously, that he was a good scholar in the Oxford sense of the word'.

Mysteriously indeed.

Edmund Gosse wrote to his wife describing a visit to Tennyson at Aldworth in August 1888, on the eve of his 79th birthday. As Gosse was leaving, Tennyson walked with him to the end of the drive.

'Never come to Marley again without coming over to see us,' he said, waving goodbye, the strange old piratical figure, tall, in black, with the flapping hat and the thick-rimmed spectacles, like a sort of vision of a superannuated highwayman.

In his book As We Were, *E.F. Benson describes a garden party at Marlborough House:*

Tennyson was seen there by Mr Oscar Browning, a Fellow of King's College, Cambridge, who had an amiable and insatiable passion for intercourse with the eminent. So he went up and shook hands with the poet. As the latter seemed to have not the slightest idea who he was, he introduced himself by saying 'I am Browning'. Tennyson must have thought he was impersonating Robert Browning, so he merely replied 'No you're not', and seemed disinclined to listen to any explanations.

In my favourite diary – that of William Allingham, who worshipped Tennyson – there is a brief entry:

After dinner Tennyson concocts an experimental punch with claret and whisky – not successful.

Although, oddly enough, something rather similar seems to have been popular with Queen Victoria. Mr Gladstone, after dining with Her Majesty, wrote to his wife:

She drank her claret strengthened, I should have thought spoiled, with whisky.

From the letters of the Rev. Sydney Smith:

Pray tell the said John Murray that three ladies apparently pregnant and much agitated have been to enquire for his direction, calling him a base, perfidious young man . . .

We now have another bed, in which a maid or a philosopher, or a maid with a philosopher, might be put. God grant that in this latter event they might both merit their respective appellations the ensuing morning.

I feel so weak, both in body and mind, that I verily believe, if the knife were put into my hand, I should not have strength or energy enough to slide it into a Dissenter.

We have had about three or four ounces of rain here, that is all. I heard of your being wet through in London, and envied you very much. The whole of this parish is pulverized from long and excessive drought. Our whole property depends on the tranquillity of the winds: if it blows before it rains, we shall all be up in the air in the shape of dust, and shall be *transparished* we know not where.

Of all modern phenomena, the most monstrous and ominous, the most manifestly rotting with disease, the most grimly prophetic of destruction, the most clearly and unmistakably inspired by evil spirits, the most instantly and awfully overshadowed by the wrath of heaven, the most near to madness and moral chaos, the most vivid with devilry and despair, is the practice of having to listen to loud music while eating a meal in a restaurant.

G.K. Chesterton

Thomas Coryat was born at Odcombe in Somerset around 1577, and was famous in his lifetime as a compulsive if distinctly eccentric traveller. According to Thomas Fuller, he 'carried folly (which the charitable called merriment) in his very face. The shape of his head had no promising form, being like a sugar-loaf inverted, with the little end before, as composed of fancy and memory without any common-sense'. Between May and October 1608 he walked the two thousand-odd miles to Venice and back, and in 1611, published Coryat's Crudities: Hastily gobled up in Five Months' Travels. He left his travel-worn shoes as a votive offering in Odcombe church (where they remained until they crumbled away to dust) and then set off, again on foot, for a journey that was to take him to Persia, Afghanistan and India – whence, alas, he never returned, dying at Surat in 1617.

Coryat aroused the insensate jealousy of another eccentric: John Taylor (1580-1654), 'the Water-poet'. Thames waterman, seaman and publican, Taylor's own pedestrian wanderings took him no further than Scotland and Germany, though in 1618 he did manage – just – to travel from London to Queenborough in a boat made of brown paper. On Coryat's death, Taylor composed not one but several epitaphs, the first and longest being apparently based on the false assumption that his old enemy had died at sea. It runs as follows:

> And now Dame *Thetis* in thy vasty womb
> Is odde Odcombian *Coriats* timelesse Tomb,
> Where *Nayads, Dryads* & sweet sea-nimphs tend him,
> And with their daily service do befriend him;
> There al-shaped *Proteus* and shrill trumping *Triton*,
> And many more which I can hardly write on,
> As if it were the thing they glory at,
> In servile troopes they wait on *Coriat*,
> That though like Hell, the sea were far more dark, as
> Yet these would guard his unregarded carkasse.
> You *Academick, Latine, Greeke Magisters*,
> You offspring of the three times treble Sisters,

Write, study, teach, until your tongues have blisters;
For now the *Haddocks* and the shifting *Sharks*
That feed on *Coriat,* will become great Clarks;
The wri-mouthed *Place,* and mumping *Whiting-Mops,*
Wil in their mawes keep *Greeke* and *Latine* shops.
The Pork-like *Porpose, Thorn-back,* and the *Scate,*
Like studious *Grecian Latinists* will prate,
And men with eating them, by inspiration,
With these two tongues shall fill each barbarous nation.
Then though the Sea hath rudely him bereft us,
Yet, midst our woes, this onely comfort's left us,
That our posterities by eating fishes,
Shall pick his wisdome out of divers dishes;
And then no doubt but thousands more will be
As learned, or perhaps as wise as he.
But to conclude, affection makes me cry,
Sorrow provokes my sleep, grief dries mine eye.

The first suggestion, I wonder, that fish is good for the brain?

From the autobiography of the cellist, Paul Tortelier:

Pau [his pianist daughter] and I gave a recital at Marlborough College in Wiltshire on a particularly pleasant autumn evening. Already during the Brahms E minor Sonata, which opened the programme, I noticed a slight shadow that flickered from time to time across the brightly lit floor. And when I began playing my own Cello Sonata I was aware of something coming towards me from above, and then floating away again. It was there, and yet not there, like an apparition. While playing, I had little time to give my attention to it, but by the time I reached the middle movement of my sonata I was able to identify my mysterious stage companion. It was a butterfly – a beautifully coloured, rather big butterfly. It began to circle around me and, as it did so, it seemed almost to be tracing arabesques to the music I was playing, its wings moving in harmony with my bow.

The audience's attention had now been drawn to this wholly unrehearsed ballet. Closer and closer the butterfly would come, almost touch me, and then fly away. It was having a flirtation with me, or perhaps I with it. The slow movement of my sonata concludes quietly on a sustained harmonic. At that moment I closed my eyes, my bow barely moving on the string. I did not want to disturb the atmosphere of peace and calm. As I slowly drew the note to an end I opened my eyes and there, perched on my left hand, was the butterfly. It had alighted so gently that I hadn't felt its presence. For a moment or two we looked at each other. It didn't move; I didn't move. It was so lovely, so ethereal, that I couldn't bring myself to shake it off. It had chosen the ideal moment for repose, I thought, settling there at the end of the slow movement; it seemed not to want to fly away. What could I do? Almost without thinking, I slowly brought my hand, with the butterfly still perched on it, up to my lips. I was sure it would fly away, but it didn't. I kissed it very tenderly, but still it didn't move. Not everyone has been able to kiss a butterfly. I never thought I would do so, least of all on the concert stage. Finally I shook my hand very gently, and it floated off into the air. That was just before the interval. After the interval we played Beethoven's A major Sonata, and there was the butterfly again, dancing all the way through, only coming down to rest from time to time on Pau's music, as if wanting to have a look at what she was doing. The piece came to an end and the butterfly was nowhere to be seen. 'Aha', I thought, 'it has left us to join the other butterflies in the fields.' Not at all. It was perched on my foot, and as the audience applauded it flapped its wings.

Who can judge what forces of spirit or nature guide our actions and bring harmony to seemingly disparate things? Such forces are there, that's all I need to know. The audience that day knew it also. We had all lived a fairy tale.

And the days are not full enough
And the nights are not full enough
And life slips by like a field mouse
Not shaking the grass

So wrote Ezra Pound in Personae *(1926). The subject is old age. The book has a nice dedication:*

> This book is for
> MARY MOORE
> of Trenton, if she
> wants it

And talking of dedications, Judith Flanders has recently come up with another gem: it is the dedication of God's Plagiarist: being an Account of the Fabulous Industry and Irregular Commerce of the Abbé Migne *by* R. Howard Block *(University of Chicago Press, 1994):*

> To the memory of Leo Lowenthal, 1900-1993
> who understood the relation
> between a life of the mind
> and drygoods

From the Times *obituary of Terence Read, barrister, April 2000:*

At Winchester Assizes in the 1950s there was a famous incident, documented in Sir James Comyn's *Watching Brief* (1993), in which the hero was the optimistic Irish barrister Terence Read. The victim was the judge, Lord Merriman, whose *D.N.B.* entry notes 'a temperament which led him at times to explosions of anger'. In 1933, in the then political mode, he had been advanced from Solicitor-General to be President of the Probate, Divorce and Admiralty Division.

For the husband in the case, Read was in the process of challenging the wife's contention that he had threatened her with a revolver. 'Look, my Lord, at the instrument which he is alleged to have used. There are even cobwebs on it now. Not used since the Crimean War, I expect.' He took up the gun and said: 'I doubt if it will ever fire.' Aiming at the bench, he then pulled the trigger.

A bullet whistled from the muzzle, missing Merriman (who dived under his desk) by inches, and lodged in the wall. The usher (later transferred) was heard to say: 'Christ, they've killed the old bugger at last.'

As regular readers of the Cracker will be aware, I have long been a fan of the American poet Phyllis McGinley. Vikram Seth is another, and has recently called my attention to

The 5:32

She said, If tomorrow my world were torn in two,
Blacked out, dissolved, I think I would remember
(As if transfixed in unsurrendering amber)
This hour best of all the hours I knew:
When cars come backing into the shabby station,
Children scuffing the seats, and the women driving
With ribbons around their hair, and the trains arriving,
And the men getting off with tired but practised motion.
Yes, I would remember my life like this, she said:
Autumn, the platform red with Virginia creeper,
And a man coming towards me, smiling, the evening paper
Under his arm, and his hat pushed back on his head;
And wood smoke lying like haze on the quiet town,
And dinner waiting, and the sun not yet gone down.

My friend Nina Lobanov has drawn my attention to this extract from The Weekend Telegraph, *January 1996:*

Euro-condoms take unity to new lengths

by Helen Cranford in Brussels

The minimum size of the Euro-condom has been decided, it was announced in Brussels last week. The minimum length is to be 6.63 inches (170mm.) and the width should be 54.56mm.

The decision follows years of negotiations after Italy proposed a uniform width of 54mm., but its northern neighbours complained that this was too small.

Experts had determined that the maximum width for a condom should be 55mm.

'One millimetre either way can make all the difference', said a Commission official at the time. 'To be blunt, it is either too tight or it comes off.' In Britain the B.S.I. standard had limited choice to either 48mm. or 52mm.

'The new rule allows a greater potential for a variety of dimensions', said Suzanne Larque, of the European Committee for Standardisation.

Most countries had national standards but with differing methods for testing, said Stewart Sanson, of the Standards Committee.

A letter from Charles Babbage (1792-1871), mathematician and inventor of the first effective calculating machine, to Alfred Lord Tennyson:

Sir,

In your otherwise beautiful poem 'The Vision of Sin' there is a verse which reads – 'Every moment dies a man, Every moment one is born.' It must be manifest that if this were true, the population of the world would be at a standstill . . .

I would suggest that in the next edition of your poem you have it read – 'Every moment dies a man, Every moment 1 1/16 is born.' The actual figure is so long I cannot get it on to a line, but I believe the figure of 1 1/16 will be sufficiently accurate for poetry.

I am, Sir, Yours etc.

Charles Babbage.

Sir Henry Halford (1766-1844) was court physician to George III, George IV, William IV and Queen Victoria, and was President of the College of Physicians from 1820 until his death. His contemporary J.F. Clarke accused him of having acquired the fourth cervical vertebra of Charles I, cut through with the axe, when the royal coffin was opened in 1813, and of subsequently passing it round at dinner-parties.

He had two favourite rules of Health:

1. Never drink claret in an east wind;
2. Never read by candlelight anything smaller than the Ace of Clubs.

(See new Bonus to the year 2005, page 208)

Here is a letter from Sir Alfred Munnings, P.R.A., to Sir William Reid Dick R.A.:

Arts Club
40 Dover Street, W. 1

January 12, 1940

My dear Reid Dick,

How to colour a bronze!

'Brown Jade' stands on the lawn against a bed of old standard roses, looking placid enough – the birds, as I feed them, pick round him on these frosty mornings and hop under his legs; whilst a rime of silver is on his back & along his neck & ears and a tiny icicle hangs from his lips. I go out and have my first pee on him; I do it lovingly and standing astride over him and guiding the warm stream along him. I leave him, wet and glistening in the early rays of the late-rising winter sun. If I'm still in the house at eleven o'clock & being, alas! a man of 60 and ready to do it again, I do it once more, having noted the green stripes the last stream has made, dry on him. Then, if I am in to lunch I walk out of the glass doors yet again – it being only three yards from the doors & then, if I come home from a walk in the dusk, with the precious [sic] light of the new sickle moon to show him up, I do it & again about 8:30 when I find him out there in the cold night with a torch. About 10:30, before I go to bed out I go again and pee on him, shutting out the light through the curtained doors, for the blackout, then I sniff the clean cold air & look up the tall old wellingtonia tree nearby & think of all the birds sleeping, heads under wings – up in the dark shadows & in the ivy & the laurels & the starlings snug and warm in the old roof. Then the spotlight of the torch shows the bronze horse to me there, all cold & chilly, always the same – ears pricked, still, and like life; although I did him. So I fumble at my flys & stand over him & trickle & trickle up and down his back until the last drop is flicked off my J.T. & so indoors & to bed.

70

In the morning, there he is again shining with ice & sparkling with frost, reflecting the red sun and looking like a 'chaser with half-dried sweat on him. The grass is all silvered and I feed the birds and down they come and peck all round him & he takes no notice of them – nor they of him & hungry seagulls whistling and stooping, are afraid to alight so near the house & later, rooks & jackdaws in the full sun and I begin already to perceive a quality of colour coming! What a business. Hope you're well –

Yours –
A

The things that claw and the things that gore
   Are unreliable things;
And so is a man with a sword in his hand,
   And rivers, and women, and kings.

The Pancatantra
(Sanskrit, 2nd century)

MISSING SNAKE TURNS UP IN TUBA

A boy's missing pet snake turned up during a tuba lesson at Malsis School, near Keighley West Yorkshire.

Matthew Duxbury, 12, of East Morton, took off the mouthpiece and out popped Sid, his 2ft-long red-sided garter snake.

Daily Telegraph
16 November 1994

This was sent me by my old friend Ken Broughshane, with the comment
Dieu, que le son du boa est triste au fond du cor . . .

{I have now noticed that precisely the same joke turns up in Nancy Mitford's The Pursuit of Love.*)*

The whole thing hangs, of course, the most famous line by Alfred de Vigny 'Dieu! que le son du cor est triste au fond des bois!' Now Quentin Blake has recently pointed out that the first punster was almost certainly a certain Maurice Donnay, author of a verse which appeared in 'Le Chat Noir' of 11 July 1891:

Un jour un grand serpent, trouvant un cor de chasse,
Pénètre dans le pavillon;
Et comme il n'avait pas beaucoup de place,
Dans l'instrument le reptile se tasse.
Mais, terrible punition!
Quand il voulait revoir le grand air et l'espace,
Et la vierge forêt au magique décor,
Il eut beau tenter maint effort,
Il ne pouvait sortir du cor,
Le pauvre boa constrictor;
Et pâle, il attendit la mort.

Moralité
Dieu! comme le boa est triste au fond du cor!

Then a change began slowly to declare itself. The horizon became clearer, field and tree came more into sight, and somehow with a different look; the mystery began to drop away from them. A bird piped suddenly, and was still; and a light breeze sprang up and set the reeds and bullrushes rustling. Rat, who was in the stern of the boat, while Mole sculled, sat up suddenly and listened with a passionate intentness. Mole, who with gentle strokes was just keeping the boat moving while he scanned the banks with care, looked at him with curiosity.

'It's gone!' sighed the Rat, sinking back into his seat again. 'So beautiful and strange and new! Since it was to end so soon, I almost wish I had never heard it. For it has roused a longing in me that is pain, and nothing seems worthwhile but just to hear that sound once more and go on listening to it for ever. No! There it is again!' he cried, alert once more. Entranced, he was silent for a long space, spellbound.

'Now it passes on and I begin to lose it,' he said presently. 'O Mole! the beauty of it! The merry bubble and joy, the thin, clear, happy call of the distant piping! Such music I never dreamed of, and the call in it is stronger even than the music is sweet! Row on, Mole, row! For the music and the call must be for us.'

The Mole, greatly wondering, obeyed. 'I hear nothing myself,' he said, 'but the wind playing in the reeds and rushes and osiers.'

Kenneth Grahame
The Wind in the Willows

When The Wind in the Willows *was first published in October 1908,* The Times *wrote:*

As a contribution to natural history, the book is negligible.

BONUS

In the 1984 Cracker I included a monologue that I had known since my childhood. It was recorded by Stanley Holloway – most famous, perhaps, for his 'Albert and the Lion' series – and it described the Battle of Hastings. The following, I suspect, may have taken up the other side of the record. The poems were actually written by a certain Marriott Edgar, the half-brother of Edgar Wallace. For best results they should be read aloud, in the broadest of Yorkshire accents.

You've 'eard of the Magna Charter,
As were signed at the Barons' command,
On Runnymede, island in t'middle of Thames,
By King John, who were known as Lackland.

Some say it were wrong of the Barons,
Their will on the King so to thrust,
But you'll see, if you look on both sides of the case,
That they 'ad to do something, or bust.

For John, from the moment they crowned 'im,
Started actin' so cunnin' and sly,
Bein' King, of course 'e couldn't do any wrong,
But by gum, he'd a proper good try.

'E squandered the rate-payers' money,
All their cattle and corn did 'e take,
Till there wasn't a morsel of bread in the land
And folks 'ad to manage on cake.

It were all right 'im bein' a tyrant
To vassals and folks of that class,
But 'e tried on 'is tricks with the Barons an' all,
And that's where 'e made a *faux pass*.

'E started bombardin' their castles
An' burnin' them over their 'ead,
Till there wasn't enough castles left to go round
And they 'ad to sleep six in a bed.

So they went to the King in a body,
And their spokesman, Fitzwalter by name,
'E opened the 'ole in 'is 'elmet,
And said, peaceful-like, 'What's the game?'

The King starts to shilly an' shally,
'E sits, an' 'e 'aws an' 'e 'ums,
Till the Barons in rage started gnashin' their teeth,
And them with no teeth gnashed their gums.

Said Fitz through the 'ole in 'is 'elmet,
'It was you who put us in this plight';
And John, 'avin' nothin' to say to this 'ere,
Murmured 'Leave your address, an' I'll write.'

This angered the gallant Fitzwalter,
'E stamped on the floor with 'is foot,
An' were startin' to give John a rare tickin'-off
When the 'ole in 'is 'elmet fell shut.

'We'll get 'im a Magna Charter',
'E said, when 'is face 'e 'ad freed,
Said the Barons, 'That's right, an' if one's not enough
Get a couple, an' 'appen they'll breed'.

They set about makin' a charter,
When at finish they'd got it drawn up,
It looked like a paper on cattle disease,
Or an entry for t'Waterloo Cup.

Next day King John, all unsuspectin',
And 'avin' the afternoon free,
To Runnymede Island 'ad taken a boat
An' were 'avin' some shrimps for 'is tea.

'E 'ad just pulled the 'ead off a big 'un,
And were pinchin' its tail with 'is thumb,
When up came a bargeload of Barons, who said,
'We thowt you'd be 'ere, so we've come.'

When they told 'im they'd brought Magna Charter,
The King seemed to go kind of limp,
But mindin' 'is manners 'e took off 'is 'at
And said 'thanks very much - 'ave a shrimp'.

'You'd best sign at once', said Fitzwalter,
'If you don't, I'll tell thee for a start,
The next coronation will 'appen quite soon,
And you won't be there to take part.'

They spread Charter out on t'tea table,
And John signed 'is name like a lamb;
('is writin' in places was sticky an' thick,
Through dippin' 'is pen in the jam.)

And it's all through that there Magna Charter
As were made by the Barons of old,
That in England today we can do what we may
Just as long as we do what we're told.

A Christmas Cracker

2002

Robert William Roper was a Fellow of Trinity College, Oxford, from 1871 until his death in 1915. During his term of office as Dean he posted up a notice outside Hall. It read as follows:

BREAD THROWING IN HALL

Gentlemen coming from homes where bread throwing at the dinner table is habitual, and finding a difficulty in conforming suddenly to the unfamiliar ways of a higher civilisation, will be permitted to continue their domestic pastime, on a payment of 5/- a throw, during their first year. After that the charge will be doubled.

From The Daily Telegraph, *28 December 1992:*

Sir,

I was interested to read (letter, December 22) that Lord Delaval Beresford died in a train collision in 1906, since his uncle, the 3rd Marquess of Waterford, once proposed to one of the first railway companies in Ireland that it should start two engines in opposite directions on the same line in order that he might witness the smash. His Lordship was, I understand, prepared to pay for his pleasure.

Among his other eccentricities, he painted the Melton Mowbray toll bar red (was this the origin of the expression 'painting the town red'?), put aniseed on the hooves of a parson's horse before hunting the terrified divine, and placed a donkey in the bed of a hapless traveller at an inn.

As for Lord Delaval's brother, Admiral Lord Charles Beresford, whom your correspondent also mentions, 'Charlie B.' had a hunt in full cry tattooed down his back, with the fox going to earth in the appropriate aperture.

Lest it be thought, however, that this fine Irish sporting dynasty were too wild for their own good, another brother, Lord William Beresford, won the V.C. in the Zulu Wars.

Thomas Byrne
Dublin

Tattoos are always good for a laugh. Judith Flanders has called my attention to a letter from Sir Edward Burne-Jones to Helen Mary Gaskell, 4 September 1894:

The lady whose shoulders are tattooed with the Last Supper is in town – is at the Aquarium – and I am going with Luke Fildes to see her. On Saturday he saw her – the tattooings are still perfect – only she is somewhat fatter, and all the faces of the Apostles are a little wider, and have a tendency to smile.

When my friends John and Sarah Riddell were living in Tokyo, their landlord left them the following questionnaire;

DAIKANYAMA PLAZA
MAINICHI FUDOSAN COMPANY LTD

To our Tenant,
 In order to improve the public health of Daikanyama Plaza and Annex. We are now preparing the basic servey for several factors related to sanitary circumstances of the building as mentioned hereinbelow. We would appreciate you for your cooperation on this by indicating your opinion by putting circles on appropriate items.
Regards, R. Watanabe

1. How about a Fly, Mosquito and Cockroach etc.?
   A. I have seen it in my room.
   B. I have seen it around the building and garbage space.
   C. haven't seen it anywhere.

2. How about a smell?
   I don't like –
   A. A smell in my room. (Please, details:)
   B. A smell of fishes of Sushi shop located 1st floor.
   C. A smell and smoke of Broiled eels of Sushi shop.
   D. A smell of Tempra shop located basement.
   E. A smell of around building. (Please, details:)
   F. Anything else? (Please, details:)
   G. I don't feel nothing.

3. How about a din?
   I don't like –
   A. A noise of a structure in my room. (Please, details:)
   B. A noise of a structure in this building. (Please, details:)
   C. A noise of trafic.
   D. A noise maked by another tenant, (ex. radio, TV set etc.)

E. A noise maked by the restaurant, (ex. noise of cooking,
    customer's going in and out, etc.)
F. Anything else? (Please, details:)
G. I don't feel nothing.

4. Please direct us anything else you find out.

A message from Kemal Atatürk to the people of Australia, written in 1934 and now inscribed on a memorial stone above Anzac Cove, Gallipoli:

Those heroes who shed their blood and lost their lives – you are now lying in the soil of a friendly country. Therefore rest in peace. There is no difference between the Johnnies and the Mehmets; to us they lie side by side, here in this country of ours. You, the mothers who sent their sons from far-away countries, wipe away your tears: your sons are now lying in our bosom and are at peace. After having lost their lives on this land of ours, they have become our sons as well.

Thoughts on a journey through Orissa, north-east India:

You're certain to like Bubaneshwar
Enormously – that is, unleshwar
    A Muslim fanatic
    Devout and dogmatic
Or under political preshwar.

We left Bubaneshwar for Puri,
Which rouses some people to furi;
    But for many a Hindu
    It opens a windu
On paradise – so, a hung juri.

And on returning to the capital:

I fear that some parts of Old Delhi
Are – let's face it – a weeny bit smelhi;
    For the rest, it's chaotic
    But rather exotic –
And just like you see on the telhi.

India is a great place for limericks. The following is not by me – I only wish it were – but by my friend, limériciste extraordinaire, – *Adam Fergusson:*

I found, when I fell off my elephant,
That waving for help was irrelephant;
    As the mahout was blind,
    With great presence of mind
I got out my mobile and telephant.

To Elizabeth Jane Howard I owe this gem, passed to her by her friend Christopher Bishop. It is a letter from his great-aunt Edith Crow to her sister Mabel. [Unfortunately the typed copy from which this is taken bears no date; Christopher's cousin Hamish is now trying to trace the original.]

My dear Mabel,

As you will be visiting us this weekend, I wonder if you would render me a little service as you come through London.

I do not in any way wish to persuade you to break your journey, but I know you have to change trains at Baker Street, and I was wondering if by any chance you would like a breath of air before resuming your journey. I am even visualising a little stroll in the Park for you – it will be very pleasant just now with the crocuses coming out.

If you decide upon this course, you will pass, I think, a Fuller's shop on your left as you walk towards the Park, and I just wondered if you would call in and get me a Mocha cake – Arthur is so fond of them and we find we cannot obtain them easily in this remote spot. One of the penalties, of course, of living in the country!

The kind of cake I want has butter icing inside, is covered with American frosting flavoured with coffee, and has decorations of burnt almonds and walnuts. They are delicious, but you have had them so often that I need not describe them – Mother so seldom let a special occasion pass without one.

On no account bring a chocolate cake – they are anathema to your brother-in-law! On the other hand there is a particularly good angel cake to which he is not indifferent, but as I know of your own preference for the Mocha cake it would seem to be the best choice.

Be sure that the icing *is* American frosting and take particular care that they pack it carefully for you – I should not like you to be embarrassed by having to produce a battered cake after your journey. I will, of course, refund anything you may spend, and on no account execute this commission unless you feel drawn to the idea of a saunter when you arrive at Baker Street after your two hours' journey. We shall look forward to your coming, with or without the cake.

Your affectionate sister
Edith

PS. On second thoughts, do not bring the cake.

THE COFFIN WORM

which consider

The worm unto his love: lo, here's fresh store;
Want irks us less as men are pinched the more.
Why dost thou lag? thou pitiest the man?
Fall to, the while I teach thee what I can.
Men in their lives full solitary be:
We are their last and kindest company.
Lo, where care's claws have been! those marks are grim;
Go, gentle love, erase the scar from him.
Hapless perchance in love (most men are so),
Our quaint felicity he could not know:
We and our generation shall show love
Throughout that frame he was not master of;
Flatter his wishful beauties; in his ear
Whisper he is at last beloved here;
Sing him (and in no false and siren strain)
We will not leave him while a shred remain
On his sweet bones: then shall our labour cease,
And the imperishable part find peace
Ever from love; meanwhile how blest he lies,
Love in his heart, his empty hands, his eyes.

Ruth Pitter (1897-1992)
A Mad Lady's Garland

And, while we're on the subject, here is a verse from the English Church Hymnal:

> Worms, strike your harp! Your voices tune
>   To sing your Maker's praise;
> Leap from the earth with pious mirth
>   And trumpet forth your lays!

This sublime quatrain came to me indirectly – through Robertson Davies – from Canon Cyril Taylor, formerly Precentor at Salisbury Cathedral. Canon Taylor suspected that it might have been concocted by Percy Dearmer when he was editing the Hymnal; but Dearmer always denied it.

Closely akin is another verse, quoted by Nicholas Parsons in The Joy of Bad Verse, *1988:*

> Ye monsters of the bubbling deep,
>   Your Maker's praises shout;
> Up the sand, ye codlings, leap,
>   And wag your tails about.

What dreadful weather we have! – It keeps one in a continual state of inelegance.

> *Jane Austen, in a letter of 18 September 1796*

Elsewhere – but I can't remember where – she writes:

Human nature is so well disposed towards those who are in interesting situations, that a young person, who either marries or dies, is sure of being kindly spoken of.

*From the address by Sir James Beament at the memorial service, held
on 31 October 1992, of the Cambridge physicist Shirley Falloon:*

. . . After the war he returned to Cambridge and worked
in the Radio Group under John Ratcliffe in the Cavendish
Laboratory. It is difficult to imagine two more disparate
characters than Falloon and Ratcliffe; indeed I am told that
Ratcliffe often referred to him, in the insurance company's
parlance, as an Act of God . . . Ratcliffe thought to defeat
Falloon's ingenuity by asking him to devise something for the
1954 Physical Society conference which would prevent even the
most distinguished speakers from over-running their time. The
sight of the device Shirley placed on the bench and known as
the Auto Cor Strike a Light so terrified speakers that it was
left to Ratcliffe's closing speech to demonstrate its awesome
properties. When the Chairman pressed a button a loud spark
lit a Bunsen burner. This heated a boiler which first blew a
whistle and then powered a steam engine which drew back a
large hammer. That in turn struck a huge tuning fork whose
vibration excited a device which switched on a low voltage
transformer. And that ignited a thunderflash. As several people
have observed, the great difference between Shirley Falloon
and Heath Robinson was that Shirley's improbable devices and
ideas not only worked, but in the best sense of the practical joke
were always carefully calculated so as never to be a danger to
anyone. For example, when the late Ken Machin was asked by
the Philharmonic Society to provide maroons in King's Chapel
for the Berlioz Funeral Pieces, it was Shirley who checked the
sums to ensure the safety of the famous windows – and who
also saw to it that when they were discharged they left behind a
fine smell of sulphur . . .

Later, he was Chairman of the University Gliding Club for
six years, during which he guided the critical negotiations that
transferred its activities from Marshall's Airport to Duxford.
Older members of that club will however remember him above
all for a particular November 5th when various gliding clubs

were invited by the Luton club to their annual party on Dunstable Downs. Each club was asked to bring a firework. The Falloon Molecular Land Mine, as it became known, did indeed start with a simple penny firework, from whose blue touch paper the igniter retired in great haste because it burned through the critical piece of string which suspended a large bucket of liquid oxygen over an open drum of petrol. The resulting explosion was seen and heard over many miles, including by the local Fire Brigade. They were not asked again.

In the 1994 Cracker I transcribed a number of items from that glorious anthology The Stuffed Owl. *If you open Bartlett's* Familiar Quotations, *1891 edition, and look up the word 'Bosom', this is what you find:*

> Bosom, cleanse the stuffed, 125
> > bears, snow white thy frozen, 49
> > come rest in this, 522
> > man take fire in his, 825
> > of God, her seat is the, 31
> > of his Father and his God, 386
> > of the ocean, buried in the, 95 . . .
> > of thy God, calm on the, 570 . . .
> > sleep in Abraham's, 97
> > slow growth in an aged, 364
> > swell, with thy fraught, 155
> > third in your, 107
> > thorns that in her, lodge, 132
> > warm cheek and rising, 382
> > was young, when my, 515
> > what, beats not, 336.

And from Miss Manners's Guide to the Rearing of Perfect Children:

> Etiquette, Sacred Subject of, 1-389

Question 3A of the application form for New York University reads: 'In order for the admissions staff of our College to get to know you, the applicant, better, we ask that you answer the following question: Are there any significant experiences you have had, or accomplishments you have realised, that have helped to define you as a person? An applicant replied:

I am a dynamic figure, often seen scaling walls and crushing ice. I have been known to remodel train stations in my lunch breaks, making them more efficient in the area of heat return. I translate ethnic slurs for Cuban refugees, I write award-winning operas, I manage time efficiently.

Occasionally, I tread water for three days in a row.

I woo women with my sensuous and godlike trombone playing, I can pilot bicycles up severe inclines with unflagging speed, and I cook thirty-minute brownies in twenty minutes. I am an expert in stucco, a veteran in love, and an outlaw in Peru.

Using only a hoe and a large glass of water, I once single-handedly defended a small village in the Amazon basin from a horde of ferocious army ants. I play bluegrass cello, I was scouted by the Mets, I am the subject of numerous documentaries. When I'm bored, I build large suspension bridges in my yard. I enjoy urban hang gliding. On Wednesdays, after school, I repair electrical appliances free of charge.

I am an abstract artist, a concrete analyst, and a ruthless bookie. Critics world-wide swoon over my original line of corduroy evening wear. I don't perspire. I am a private citizen, yet I receive fan mail. I have been caller number nine and have won the weekend passes. Last summer I toured New Jersey with a travelling centrifugal-force demonstration. I bat 400.

My deft floral arrangements have earned me fame in international botany circles. Children trust me.

I can hurl tennis rackets at small moving objects with deadly accuracy. I once read *Paradise Lost, Moby Dick* and *David Copperfield* in one day and still had time to refurbish an entire dining room that evening. I know the exact location of every food item in the supermarket. I have performed several covert operations with the CIA. I sleep once a week; when I do sleep, I sleep in a chair. While on vacation in Canada, I successfully negotiated with a group of terrorists who had seized a small bakery. The laws of physics do not apply to me.

I balance, I weave, I dodge, I frolic, and my bills are all paid. On weekends, to let off steam, I participate in full-contact origami. Years ago I discovered the meaning of life but forgot to write it down. I have made extraordinary four-course meals using only a mouli and a toaster oven.

I breed prize-winning clams. I have won bullfights in San Juan, cliff-diving competitions in Sri Lanka, and spelling bees at the Kremlin.

I have played Hamlet, have performed open-heart surgery, and have spoken with Elvis.

But I have not yet gone to college.

He got in.

Two magnificent dicta of Queen Victoria:

The Queen is most anxious to enlist every one who can speak or write to join in checking this mad, wicked folly of 'Woman's Rights', with all its attendant horrors, on which her poor feeble sex is bent, forgetting every sense of womanly feeling and propriety.

The second comes in a letter to her granddaughter Princess Victoria of Hesse, dated 22 August 1883:

I would earnestly warn you against trying to find out the reason for and explanation of everything . . . To try and find out the reason for everything is very dangerous and leads to nothing but disappointment and dissatisfaction, unsettling your mind and in the end making you miserable.

'Rich soil', remarked the landlord.
'Lavishly watered. Streams to the right,
Fountains on the left.
The rose, you observe, is without a thorn.'

'What's a thorn?' asked Adam.
'Something you have in your side,'
The landlord replied.

'And since there are no seasons
All the flowers bloom all the time.'

'What's a season?' Eve inquired.
'Yours not to reason why'
The landlord made reply.

Odours rose from the trees,
Grapes fell from the vines,
The sand was made of gold,
The pebbles were made of pearls.

'I've never seen the like', said Eve.
'Naturally', the landlord smiled.

'It's unimaginable!' sighed Adam.
'You're not obliged to imagine it'
Snapped the landlord. 'Yet.'

D.J. Enright

A corrigendum slip in the Australian Dictionary of National Biography reads:

For 'died in infancy' read 'lived to a ripe old age at Orange.'

Another, from an unknown American newspaper, is quoted by Edward Burne-Jones – there he is again – in a letter to Lady Horner and recorded in Geoffrey Madan's Notebooks:

Instead of being arrested, as we stated, for kicking his wife down a flight of stairs and hurling a lighted kerosene lamp after her, the Revd. James P. Wellman died unmarried four years ago.

In a letter to The Times *in September 1997, Professor B. Brinkworth, F.Eng., wrote of his own favourite:*

CORRIGENDUM
to
One-hundred-and-eleventh Report
of the Engineering Physics Sub-Committee
Aeronautical Research Council
Page 1, 4th line from bottom of the page:
delete 'possible', insert 'impossible'.

He ends the letter:

The (somewhat embarrassed) Secretary of the Sub-Committee at the time was

Yours faithfully,
Brian Brinkworth

Magical single lines? I have long been haunted by Yeats's

 And all dishevelled wandering stars

Auden wrote another, of Yeats himself:

 Mad Ireland hurt you into poetry.

Karel Capek on Madame Tussaud's:

Madame Tussaud's is a museum of famous people, or rather of their wax effigies. The Royal Family is there (also King Alphonso, somewhat moth-eaten). Mr MacDonald's ministry, French Presidents, Dickens and Kipling, marshals, Mademoiselle Lenglen, famous murderers of the last century and souvenirs of Napoleon, such as his socks, belt and hat; then in a place of dishonour Kaiser Wilhelm and Franz Josef, still looking spruce for his age. Before one particularly effective effigy of a gentleman in a top-hat I stopped and looked into the catalogue to see who it was; suddenly the gentleman with the top-hat moved and walked away; it was awful. After a while two young ladies looked into the catalogue to see whom I represented. At Madame Tussaud's I made a somewhat unpleasant discovery: either I am quite incapable of reading human faces, or else physiognomies are deceptive. So for example I was at first sight attracted by a seated gentleman with a goatee beard, No. 12. In the catalogue I found: '12. Thomas Neill Cream, hanged in 1892. Poisoned Matilda Glover with strychnine. He was also found guilty of murdering three other women.' Really, his face is very suspicious. No. 13, Franz Muller, murdered Mr Briggs on the train. H'm. No. 20, a clean-shaven gentleman, of almost worthy appearance: Arthur Devereux, hanged 1905, known as the 'trunk murderer' because he hid the corpses of his victims in trunks. Horrid. No. 21 – no, this worthy priest cannot be 'Mrs Dyer, the Reading baby murderess.' I now perceive that I have confused the pages of the catalogue, and I am compelled to correct my impressions: the seated gentleman, No. 12, is merely Bernard Shaw; No. 13 is Louis Bleriot, and No. 20 is simply Guglielmo Marconi.

Never again will I judge people by their faces.

Letters from England.

Elsewhere he writes:

Wales is the land of mountains, Lloyd George, trout, excursionists, jackdaws, slate, castles, rain, bards and a Celtic language. The mountains are bald and violet-coloured, strange and full of stones; in the hotels there are moist photographs of organizers of singing contests, which are a sort of national speciality; Welsh sheep have long tails, and if you were to cut me into pieces, that is all I know about North Wales. If anybody thinks this is not much, well, he had better go to Carnarvon. Change at Bangor.

In the 1974 Cracker I included the famous Dictée, *set one evening by Prosper Mérimée to the court of Napoleon III at Fontainebleau, which was always said to be the most difficult French dictation ever devised. As I pointed out at the time, the Emperor himself made forty-five mistakes, Empress Eugénie sixty-two – which was thought not bad for a Spaniard. Perhaps because of this, in June 1992 I was asked to preside over the second* Championnats d'orthographe franco-britanniques *at the French Lycée in London, at which some two hundred people competed in a dictation read by the French Ambassador. It was nowhere near as difficult as Mérimée's – I think I made three mistakes, though there might have been more – but to settle the matter between the several finalists who had made no mistakes at all –* pour départager les ex aequo, *as it was rather charmingly put – the following two additional sentences were added:*

Dans un de ces bric-à-brac faits de brie et de broc, des boute-en-train et des boutefeux, après s'être pris à bras-le-corps, s'étaient fait des baisemains, s'étaient récité des bouts-rimés avant de se remettre en quête, clopin-clopant, d'objets les plus divers: des brise-bise, des boutons-pression, des passe-thé, des hauts-de-forme et des tableaux embus.

Une polyglotte falote mais fiérote vivant dans une paillote, et ayant pour mascotte une haridelle étique, rêvait en regardant sur l'écran un carroussel où un cavalier sonnait l'hallali pour obtenir la reddition d'une ennemie félonne qui faisait la chattemite en jouant de l'ocarina.

Talking of Mérimée, it's perhaps worth mentioning that when he wrote his story Carmen – *which was to inspire Georges Bizet's opera – he had never been to Spain.* 'Ecrivons un livre sur l'Espagne', *he said,* 'et avec l'argent que le livre nous gagne, allons en Espagne pour voir si ce que nous avons écrit est vrai.'

Or, if anyone would like a translation, 'Let us write a book about Spain, and with the money the book makes us let us go to Spain to see if what we have written is true.'

'[*I have retained this last little story because I am honour-bound to do so, but it pains me to record that on 2 December 2002 my old friend Stuart Preston wrote to me from Paris:* 'Mérimée first went to Spain in 1830. He (a hero of mine) wrote 'Carmen' in 1845. Between those dates he frequently visited Madrid, the opening scene of his long amitié amoureuse with Madame de Montijo, the Empress Eugénie's mother. Voilà!'*]*'

Some genius has discovered that 'President Clinton of the USA' has interesting anagram:

To copulate, he finds interns.

But better yet is an anagram of

To be or not to be: that is the question.
Whether 'tis nobler in the mind to suffer
The slings and arrows of outrageous fortune . . .

which turns out to be

In one of the Bard's best-thought-of tragedies,
our insistent hero, Hamlet, queries on two
fronts about how life turns rotten.

To see the world properly you should not think of it as worse or better than it is. Love and hatred are closely connected, and both distort our vision. The thing to do is to look at everything as attentively as possible, to inscribe all things in our memory, never to let a day go by without acquiring something. Then to apply oneself to those branches of knowledge which give the mind a definite direction, to compose things, to determine values – that is what we have to do now. At the same time we must not want to *be* something but strive to *become* everything; and, especially, we must not stand still and rest more often than the weariness of mind and body demands.

That extract is from a letter by Goethe, 24 August 1772, to a Frankfurt schoolboy who had written to him for advice. He himself was 22 years old.

His mother remembered his childhood:

Air, fire, water and earth I presented to him as beautiful princesses, and everything in all nature took on a deeper meaning. We invented roads between stars, and what great minds we would encounter . . . He devoured me with his eyes; and if the fate of one of his favourites did not go as he wished, this I could see from the anger in his face, or his efforts not to break out in tears. Occasionally he interfered by saying: 'Mother, the princess will *not* marry the miserable tailor, even if he slays the giant,' at which I stopped and postponed the catastrophe until the next evening. So my imagination often was replaced by his; and when the following morning I arranged fate according to his suggestions and said: 'You guessed it, that's how it came out,' he was all excited, and one could see his heart beating.

And oh, what a confection of delights you find in a glass of this Brouilly! A daisy-like floweriness coddled in the almondy scents of a Bakewell tart assaults you at a sniff. There's a rubberiness, yes, as you would expect, but high-class rubber, make no mistake. Take a swig (for, despite the price, this remains essentially a swigging wine) and in roar the cherry fruits. There's a touch of cream, a stab of pepper . . . even a faint edge of cheese. It's a serious example of a marvellously unserious wine.

The Mail on Sunday Magazine

My paternal grandfather was, I learn from the O.E.D., a nimgimmer
– 'a Doctor, Surgeon or Apothecary, or anyone that cures a Clap or
the Pox'. Here, slightly abridged but in no way censored, is his entry
in the old D.N.B.:

COOPER, Sir Alfred (1838-1908), surgeon, born at Norwich on
28 Dec. 1838, was son of William Cooper, at one time recorder of
Ipswich, by his wife Anne Marsh . . . In 1858 Cooper entered as a
student at St Bartholomew's Hospital. He was admitted M.R.C.S.
England on 29 June 1861[1]. He then went to Paris in company with
(Sir) Thomas Smith to improve his anatomical knowledge, and on
his return was appointed a prosector to the examiners at the Royal
College of Surgeons.

Cooper started practice in Jermyn Street. After an interval of
waiting he acquired a fashionable private practice. But his social
success rather stimulated than retarded his ardour for surgery. He
was surgeon to St Mark's Hospital for Fistula, City Road, from
April 1864 to 1897 . . . and to the Lock Hospital, Soho. At the last
institution he gained that sound knowledge of syphilis with which his
name is chiefly associated . . .

Cooper, whose social qualities were linked with fine traits of
character and breadth of view, gained a wide knowledge of the
world, partly at courts, partly in the out-patient rooms of hospitals,
and partly in the exercise of a branch of his profession which more
than any other reveals the frailty of mankind . . .

Cooper's works are: 1. *Syphilis and Pseudo-Syphilis,* 1884; 2nd
edn. 1895[2]. 2. *A Practical Treatise on Disease of the Rectum,* 1887;
2nd edn., with Mr F. Swinford Edwards, entitled *Diseases of the*
Rectum and Anus, 1892.

Perhaps not altogether surprisingly, he numbered King Edward
VII among his patients. He married above himself: Lady Agnes
Duff was the daughter of the fifth Earl of Fife. Alas, by the time
she met Dr Cooper at the age of twenty-eight she had notched up

two elopements and a divorce. It was said that together they knew more about the private parts of the British aristocracy than any other couple in the country. I am proud to be their grandson.

¹ Three years' training seems to have been thought enough in those days.
² I am the proud possessor of a copy of this, profusely illustrated in colour, but I show it only to those of sturdy constitution – and never after dinner.

The morning stars sang together, and all the sons of God shouted for joy.

Job, xxxviii, 7.

BONUS

Dunkirk

Will came back from school that day,
And he had little to say.
But he stood a long time looking down
To where the grey-green Channel water
Slapped at the foot of the little town,
And to where his boat, the *Sarah P*,
Bobbed at the tide on an even keel,
With her one old sail patched at the leech,
Furled like a slattern down at heel.

He stood for a while above the beach,
He saw how the wind and current caught her:
He looked a long time out to sea.
There was steady wind, and the sky was pale,
And a haze in the east that looked like smoke.

Will went back to the house to dress.
He was half-way through, when his sister Bess
Who was near fourteen, and younger than he
By just two years, came home from play.
She asked him, 'Where are you going, Will?'
He said 'For a good long sail.'

'Can I come along?' 'No, Bess', he spoke.
'I may be gone for a night and a day.'
Bess looked at him. She kept very still.
She had heard the news of the Flanders rout,
How the English were trapped above Dunkirk,
And the fleet had gone to get them out -
But everyone thought that it wouldn't work.

There was too much fear, there was too much doubt.

She looked at him, and he looked at her.
They were English children, born and bred.
He frowned her down, but she wouldn't stir.
She shook her proud young head.
'You'll need a crew,' she said.

They raised the sail on the *Sarah P*,
Like a penoncel on a young knight's lance,
And headed the *Sarah* out to sea
To bring their soldiers home from France.

There was no command, there was no set plan,
But six hundred boats went out with them
On the grey-green waters, sailing fast,
River excursion and fisherman,
Tug and schooner and racing M,
And the little boats came following last.

From every harbor and town they went
Who had sailed their craft in the sun and rain,
From the South Downs, from the cliffs of Kent,
From the village street, from the country lane.

There are twenty miles of rolling sea
From coast to coast, by the seagull's flight,
But the tides were fair and the wind was free,
And they raised Dunkirk by the fall of night.

They raised Dunkirk with its harbor torn
By the blasted stern and the sunken prow;
They had raced for fun on an English tide,
They were English children bred and born,
And whether they lived, or whether they died,
They raced for England now.

Bess was as white as the Sarah's sail,
She set her teeth and she smiled at Will.
He held his course for the smoky veil
Where the harbor narrowed thin and long.
The British ships were firing strong.

He took the *Sarah* into his hands,
He drove her in through fire and death
To the wet men waiting on the sands.
He got his load and he got his breath,
And she came about, and the wind fought her.

He shut his eyes and he tried to pray.
He saw his England where she lay,
The wind's green home, the sea's proud daughter,
Still in the moonlight, dreaming deep,
The English cliffs, and the English loam -
He had fourteen men to get away,
And the moon was clear, and the night like day
For planes to see where the white sails creep
Over the black water.

He closed his eyes and he prayed for her;
He prayed to the men who had made her great,
Who had built her land of forest and park,
Who had made the seas an English lake;
He prayed for a fog to bring the dark;
He prayed to get home for England's sake.
And the fog came down on the rolling sea,
And covered the ships with English mist.
The diving planes were baffled and blind.

For Nelson was there in the *Victory*,
With his one good eye, and his sullen twist,
And guns were out on the *Golden Hind*,
Their shot flashed over the *Sarah P*,
He could hear them cheer as he came about.

By burning wharves, by battered slips,
Galleon, frigate and brigantine,
The old dead Captains fought their ships,
And the great dead admirals led the line.
It was England's night, it was England's sea.
The fog rolled over the harbor key.
Bess held to the stays, and conned him out.

And all through the dark, while the *Sarah*'s wake
Hissed behind him, and vanished in foam,
There at his side sat Francis Drake,
And held him true, and steered him home.

Robert Nathan

This poem was written by a passionately anglophile American, whom I knew when he was in his nineties. It was hugely popular when I was an eleven-year-old evacuee in New York. Perhaps for that reason, I've always rather loved it; and it still brings tears to my eyes.

A
Christmas
Cracker

 2003

On 14 November 2001, Mr J.W. Thirsk wrote to The Times:

Sir,

At the Metropolitan Tabernacle, London, in 1874, a Dr Pentecost had said that he felt it his duty to give up smoking. The Baptist preacher Charles Haddon Spurgeon, speaking after him, said:

> Notwithstanding what Brother Pentecost has said, I intend to smoke a good cigar to the glory of God before I go to bed tonight. If anybody can show me in the Bible the command 'Thou shalt not smoke', I am ready to keep it; but I haven't found it yet. I find ten commandments and it's as much as I can do to keep them; and I've no desire to make them into eleven or twelve.

At twenty-two, Spurgeon was the most popular preacher of his day. The Metropolitan Tabernacle in Newington Causeway, opened in 1861, accommodated six thousand people; according to the Dictionary of National Biography, when he preached at the Surrey Gardens Music Hall, his congregation numbered ten thousand. (And this was of course in the days before sound amplification had been thought of.) A contemporary observer wrote that at the Tabernacle

> The crowd was so immense that seat holders could not get to their seats. Half an hour before time the aisles were solid blocks and many stood throughout the service, wedged in by their fellows and prevented from escaping by the crowd outside, who sealed up the doors and filled up the yard in front and stood in throngs as far as the eye could reach.

To quote the D.N.B. again (directly this time):

> During the latter part of his life he lived in some style at Norwood. He never practised or affected to practise asceticism, but was generous in the use of the ample means with which his

congregation supplied him . . .

His humour was spontaneous; it marked his private as well as his public utterances.

It is perhaps worth reminding the reader of what Lytton Strachey wrote about Cardinal Wiseman (for a fuller text see the 1978 Cracker):

. . . There was, indeed, only one point in which he resembled Bishop Blougram – his love of a good table. Some of Newman's disciples were astonished and grieved to find that he sat down to four courses of fish during Lent. 'I am sorry to say', remarked one of them afterwards, 'that there is a lobster salad side to the Cardinal.'

Probable arguments are like little starres, every one of which will be useless as to our conduct and enlightening, but when they are tyed together by order and vicinity by the finger of God and the hand of an Angel, they make a Constellation, and are not onely powerful in their influence, but like a bright Angel to guide and enlighten our way.

This lovely passage comes from Ductor Dubitantium *by the Rev. Jeremy Taylor, published in 1660. When his baby son died, he wrote to his friend John Evelyn:*

Deare Sir, I am in some little disorder by reason of the death of a little child of mine, a boy that lately made us very glad: but now he rejoyces in his little orbe, while we thinke, and sigh, and long to be as safe as he is.

In 1838 *there was published a book entitled* A Visit to the British Museum, *in dialogue form. Here is a short extract:*

What are those wooden instruments, somewhat like cricket bats, arranged round the closed door opposite to that at which we entered?

They are war-clubs or maces. Above Case the 21st are wooden pillows, and a capacious cava bowl.

You pointed out some to us before; pray what is the article that gives its name to the bowl?

Cava is an exhilarating liquor, used by the people of the Friendly Islands, as we use ale or wine, as a refreshing and, taken to excess, an intoxicating beverage. The mode of its preparation, which happens to be not over-delicate, you may read at home.

Some twenty years later, Pleasant Mornings at the British Museum, or Memorials of Bygone Ages *was published by the Religious Tract Society:*

Well, Frank, you have seen around you the evidence of heathenism abroad – come and see that of Britain; we must come back through this room and can examine its other cases then.

Oh, aunt, I can hardly fancy heathenism in Britain.

Nevertheless my dear, in this collection of British antiquities, you will find ample proof that some of our ancestors were very little better than Sandwich Islanders.

Really, aunt, it makes me quite melancholy to see these testimonies of our own civilised Britain being the home of noble savages.

I do not think that we must consider the Druidical times so entirely savage, my boy. But we will pass on to the dawn of brighter days indicated by these Roman relics.

But these are only relics of our conquerors!

We need not regard them sorrowfully, my dear boy, but with thankful remembrance how God overruled Roman ambition for British enlightenment.

Mr Francis Wright tells me of a printed notice which appeared on the gates of Postman's Park in the City of London during June 2002:

Postman's Park is closed until further notice.

This is to allow a sparrowhawk chick to fledge undisturbed, having left the nest early and committed itself to ground dwelling.

We apologise for any inconvenience caused and anticipate that the garden will be open within the next few days.

City Gardens
Corporation of London

The famous French cocotte Liane de Pougy produced a delightful diary which she called Mes cahiers bleus, *'My Blue Notebooks'. Here is the entry for 11 January 1920:*

Comme tous les matins, j'ai pris ce que nos aïeules appelaient leur 'bouillon pointu' pour la conservation de leur teint clair et de leur haleine fraîche. Habitude de famille et conseil du docteur Pinard. Une vieille grande-tante de maman, la belle Mme Rhomès, est morte à quatre-vingt-dix-huit ans et demi avec une peau de lis et de roses, un teint d'enfant. Elle s'administrait, paraît-il, tous les soirs vers 5 heures, afin de goûter un sommeil très calme, son petit bouillon pointu. Elle le faisait avec désinvolture en société. Elle se plaçait simplement devant la cheminée; la préposée arrivait discrètement avec la syringue toute amorcée; Mme Rhomès se penchait gracieusement en avant, la large robe se soulevait, un, deux, trois, c'était fait! La conversation n'avait pas cessé et ma belle ancêtre s'éclipsait au bout de quelques minutes pour de courts instants, revenant avec la satisfaction du devoir accompli.

[As every morning, I took what our ancestors called their 'pointed broth' (enema), to preserve a clear skin and sweet breath. It is a family habit, approved by Dr Pinard. One of my mother's old great-aunts, the beautiful Mme Rhomès, died at the age of ninety-eight and a half with a skin of lilies and roses, the complexion of a child. She took her little 'pointed broth', it seems, at five o'clock every evening, to ensure calm sleep. She did it cheerfully in public. She would simply stand in front of the fireplace; her maid would come in discreetly, armed with the loaded syringe; Mme Rhomès would lean forward gracefully so that her full skirts were lifted, one, two, three, and it was done! Conversation was not interrupted, and after a few minutes my beautiful ancestress would briefly disappear, soon to return with the satisfaction of a duty performed.]

Liane was the daughter of a captain in the lancers. She had been married at sixteen to a naval officer, but the marriage had been stormy from the start. One day, in a fit of doubtless well-justified jealousy, he fired two revolver shots at her. Both were hits – but both, fortunately, got her in the behind. To all but a privileged few, her beauty remained unspoilt.

The Roman Centurion's Song

(Roman Occupation of Britain, AD 300)

Legate, I heard the news last night, the cohort ordered home
By ship to Portus Itius and thence by road to Rome.
I've marched the companies aboard, the arms are stowed below:
Now let another take my sword. Command me not to go!

I've served in Britain forty years, from Vectis to the Wall.
I have none other home than this, nor any life at all.
Last night I did not understand, but now the hour draws near
That calls me to my native land, I feel that land is here.

Here where men say my name was made, here where my work was done,
Here where my dearest dead are laid – my wife – my wife and son;
Here where time, custom, grief and toil, age, memory, service, love,
Have rooted me in British soil. Ah, how can I remove?

For me this land, that sea, these airs, those folk and fields suffice.
What purple southern pomp can match our changeful Northern skies,
Black with December snows unshed or pearled with August haze –
The clanging arch of steel-grey March or June's long-lighted days?

You'll follow widening Rhodanus till vine and olive lean
Aslant before the sunny breeze that sweeps Nemausus clean
To Arelate's triple gate; but let me linger on,
Here where our stiff-necked British oaks confront Euroclydon!

You'll take the old Aurelian Road through shore-descending pines,
Where, blue as any peacock's neck, the Tyrrhene Ocean shines.
You'll go where laurel crowns are won, but – will you e'er forget
The scent of hawthorn in the sun, or bracken in the wet?

Let me work here for Britain's sake – at any task you will –
A marsh to drain, a road to make or native troops to drill.
Some western camp (I know the Pict) or granite border keep
Mid seas of heather derelict, where our old messmates sleep.

Legate, I come to you in tears – My cohort ordered home!
I've served in Britain forty years. What should I do in Rome?
Here is my heart, my soul, my mind – the only life I know.
I cannot leave it all behind. Command me not to go!

Rudyard Kipling

Rhodanus: the Rhône.
Nemausus: Nîmes.
Arelate: Arles.
Euroclydon: 'A tempestuous wind' *(Acts,* xxvii, 14)

I was told last night that the scene of noise and uproar which the House of Commons now exhibits is perfectly disgusting. This used not to be the case in better, or at least more gentlemanlike, times; no noises were permissible but the cheer and the cough, the former admitting every variety of intonation expressive of admiration, assent, denial, surprise, indignation, menace, sarcasm. Now all the musical skill of this instrument is lost and drowned in shouts, hootings, groans, noises of the most discordant that the human throat can emit, sticks and feet beating against the floor. Sir Hedworth Williamson, a violent whig, told me that there were a set of fellows on his side of the House whose regular practice it was to make this uproar, and with the settled design to bellow Peel down. This is the reformed House of Commons.

Charles Greville
4 *April* 1835

He in a few minutes ravished this fair creature, or at least would have ravished her, if she had not, by a timely compliance, prevented him.

Henry Fielding

From a Portuguese-English phrase-book, by Pedro Carlino, published in 1869:

Preface
We expect then, who the little book (for the care what we wrote him, and for her typographical correction) that may be worth the acceptation of studious persons, and especially of the Youth, at which we dedicate him particularly.

Familiar Phrases

Á quê hóras sê jânta?	At what o'clock dine him?
Toucái-vos ôu tôuque-se.	Dress your hairs.
Núnca devêmos zombár dôs infelizes.	It must never to laugh of the unhappies.
Vôs cantáis ôu Vm. cânta múito bêm.	You sing not very deal well.
Estôu encatarroádo ôu endefluxádo.	I am catched cold.

Idiotisms and Proverbs

Por dinheiro baila o perro.	Nothing some money, nothing of Swiss.
Vále pesádo â ôuro.	He is valuable his weight's gold.
A cavallo dado não se lhe olha para o dente.	A horse baared don't look him the tooth.
Pedra movediça nunca mofo a cubiça.	The stone as roll not heap up not foam.
Não tem eira, nem ramo de figueira.	He is beggar as a church rat.

Familiar Dialogue

Vènho vêr ôs sêus môveis.	I come to see yours furniture
quêro mobilér um aposênto.	I have a apartement to furnish.

123

Aquí achará Vm tôdos ôs dê quê precisar.

You will find to my store house whole that you won't.

Êsse tráste dê salão, côm damásco cramesin, é compléto?

Is it complete this parlour in damask crimson?

Não me parêce nôvo.

It seems no me new.

Tal não diga: sáhe dâs mãos dô fabricânte.

Pardon me, it comes workman's hands.

Têm Vm. espêlhos?

Have you some glasses?

Dê quê tamânho ôs quér?

Which hightness want you its?

Dê quátro pés, sêus pollegádas dê lárgo, ê sétte d'altúra, pôuco máis ôu mênos.

I want almost four feet six thumbs wide's, over seven of long.

A sad little poem by Robert Nathan:

> The world that now, in my old age,
> I go about in,
> Is not the world I was born into
> Or in which I grew up. It is a world
> Changed like the sea in another light,
> A storm light. A world
> Of raging waves and sudden terror,
> Anger…….. and fright.
> Legends are lost here, lost and forgotten.
> There is no magic here, no ardor –
> The full heart, the spirit uplifted –
> Its songs are harsh, the sound is deafening.
> The young die quickly, without love,
> Thrown to the sharks.
> We were few, but there were lions among us,
> And singing birds.
> This is a new world, without beauty,
> Without music, without rules
> And everyone is writing,
> Telling it like it is, making remarks,
> And their books are read by millions,
> In the drug stores, in the libraries, the schools.
> But there is no pride of lions in this world,
> No exultation of larks.

In previous Crackers I have quoted a number of good beginnings to books. Here is another splendid opening that I have recently come across. It is from the unattractively-named – but hugely enjoyable – novel Bumface, *by the Australian author Morris Gleitzman:*

'Angus Solomon', sighed Mrs Lowry. 'Is that a penis you've drawn in your exercise book?'

Angus jumped, startled, and remembered where he was.

Mrs Lowry was standing next to his desk, staring down at the page. Other kids were sniggering.

Angus felt his mouth go dry, and his heart speed up. For a second he thought about lying. He decided not to.

'No, Miss,' he admitted, 'it's a submarine.'

Mrs Lowry nodded grimly. 'I thought as much', she said. Now stop wasting time and draw a penis like I asked you to.' She pointed to the one she'd drawn on the blackboard.

*My dear friends Leon and Cynthia Polsky have sent me this extract
from a German hotel guide:*

PFLAUM'S POSTHOTEL PEGNITZ, Nürberger Str. 14, 27
km. S. of Bayreuth and a favourite retreat for visitors to the
Festspiel, is the most imaginative hotel in Germany, one giving
life to a soaring artistic vision. The 11th generation of Pflaums
operates the hotel. The four brothers handle all aspects: one's
a chef, another is the hotel manager, the third is the architect,
the fourth is the butcher. PPP, as it is fondly known, may look
traditional outside – half-timbered façade, gabled slate roof –
but inside is another world, or, perhaps, another galaxy. Past
carpeting layered with sand, beyond a vinyl blow-up doll
with the face from Edvard Munch's 'The Scream', guests enter
into a dark lounge where a big-screen TV beams Wagnerian
performances of yore. Internet-linked PCs line the bar. Black
spray-painted art mimics graffiti. (What would Pflaum forebears
think?) The strange lobby is often unmanned, compounding the
impersonal high-concept feel . . . .

Standard rooms – and remember that nothing here is very
standard – vary from opulent renditions of Franconian rusticity
to chic quarters decked with gingham ruffles to avant-garde
dens done in metallic grey on grey on grey . . . One has a
whirlpool tub in a bedroom, rimmed with a beach of simulated
sand and a starry false sky twinkling overhead. Another suite,
red on red with a paisley canopy, looks like Dracula's lair, while
Bacchanal, a midnight blue number, spotlights the Venetian
palace emblazoned on the wall behind the bed. Mirrors and
creative lighting intensify the hyperbole. Placido Domingo
inspired the *Parsifal Suite*, and it is Michael Jackson's favourite.
John Travolta prefers *Venus in Blue*. Travellers comfortable
with audacious aesthetics will be tickled pink, while others
may scream like that vinyl blow-up doll and flee this genuinely
perplexing, startlingly original hotel.

My stepson Guy Milford has passed on to me this wistful little poem.
We first thought it to be by the late Lord Hailsham; but I have since
learnt that the author is Elizabeth Wordsworth (1840-1932), great-
niece of William and founder of both Lady Margaret Hall and St
Hugh's College at Oxford:

> If all the good people were clever
> And all clever people were good,
> The world would be nicer than ever
> We thought that it possibly could;
>
> But somehow it's seldom or never
> The two hit it off as they should –
> The good are so harsh to the clever,
> The clever so rude to the good.
>
> 'So, friends, let it be our endeavour
> To make each by each understood,
> For few can be good like the clever,
> Or clever, so well as the good.'

(When I included only the first two verses in the 2003 Cracker I did
not know that there was a third, nor that my version was not quite
accurate. I am grateful to Mark Tennant and John Byrne for setting
me right.)

A letter to the Daily Telegraph *from Mrs Pamela Hatt of Berkhamsted, published on 3 June 1997:*

Sir,

Some time ago, when I applied for a new driving licence, it was posted to me as Mrs Watt. I sent it back, with the request: 'Please note that my name is Hatt, not Watt.' Back it came – addressed to Mrs Hattno Twatt. They did get it right the third time.

I am reminded of that wonderful day when I received a letter addressed to the Discount Norwich. It made my week.

I *always look forward to Wednesday morning, because that is the day that* The Times *publishes its weekly piece by Alan Coren. This one came out shortly before Christmas.*

WE THREE KINGS

When men steel themselves to do the Christmas shopping, they generally do it all at the last minute, buying the first thing they see.

Which at last sheds all the light we scholars have been seeking on the mysterious case of the Three Kings of Orientar, and the bizarre gifts they brought with them to Bethlehem.

For most of you, the actual geographical location of Orientar must be a mystery that has nagged annually at you down the long carolling years, but research has now led us to the belief that Orientar is in fact a rhyme-induced abbreviation of *Orient 'R'Us*, a supermarket chain specializing in such products as kaftans, spice-racks, hookahs and brass gongs.

Very much the sort of portmanteau establishment to appeal to last-minute male shoppers stuck with the problem of finding gifts for a faraway family of which they know little. Earlier, the three monarchs must have sat down and made imaginative lists. Joseph's a carpenter, isn't he, so perhaps a state-of-the-art toolbox, a multi-purpose drill, possibly a folding work-bench, what do you think, Melchior? Now what about Mary? Lingerie's always a winner – you can't go wrong with a nightie. Remember: she'll have had the baby by then; wide choice there: romper-suits, bouncer, pull-along duck . . .

But when they get to the shops – decisions! There are 87 different sorts of toolbox on show and 23 assorted folding work-benches. Lingerie emporia offer hundreds of different nighties; which material, which colour, what's her size? You go in, Caspar. Why me? What do I know about women's thingies?

Let's get the baby's present first. Blimey! Look at that! Toy shops are packed – millions of screaming kids. Let's go and have a drink and come back later when they're not so busy.

And do they come back? No, of course they don't. Across the road from the pub is the local branch of *Orient 'R' Us*.

Oh look, guys, spot on – we can get everything we want here; so in they go. And while, of course, they find no power tools, no nighties, no baby bouncers, there's gold, always an acceptable gift, Caspar, and frankincense, can't go wrong with female fragrances, Melchior, and what's that box next to it? The label says myrrh, what's myrrh when it's at home? Who cares, Balthazar, what does it matter, he's only a kid.

Sir James Richards on John Betjeman, when they were colleagues on
The Architectural Review:

He practised at that time an undergraduate style of exhibitionism which was tolerable because accompanied by wit and good humour. I remember as an example of the kind of prank he took pride in, his boasting to me one day that he had just come from the Geological Museum, then housed in a dusty, unvisited red-brick building in Piccadilly, by Pinnethorne, and had contributed an exhibit of his own. 'Do go and look', he said. So I went, and there indeed beneath the glass of one of the show-cases, which someone had I suppose carelessly left unlocked, was a small brown object with a neatly lettered card reading 'Horse Chestnut picked up in Bushey Park. Donated by J. Betjeman Esquire.' I believe it remained unnoticed and undisturbed until the building was demolished in 1935 to make way for Simpson's store.

One of the first Betjeman poems, which he loved to recite, ran as follows:

When the moors are pink with heather
When the sky's as blue as the sea,
Marching all together
Come fairy folk so wee.

And talking of John Betjeman, I can't resist quoting the love letter he received from his fiancée – and later his wife – Penelope Chetwode early in 1933. Though neither of them spoke a word of the language, it amused them occasionally to revert to the Greek alphabet.

You are a silly little boy to go on as you do about me not lovin you. You seem to have complexes about yourself and what-not. You certainly do smell very bad & are as yellow as a Quattro-cento Florentine, & you have earwigs in your nose which would revolt many people, but you must surely know by now that these defects only serve to enhance your charms in my sight, you στινχιν γελλοψ τρεασυρε [stinkin yellow treasure].

Due reverence ought to be shown to my body at my funeral having regard to the fact that during its life it was the Temple of the Holy Ghost. At the same time this reverence ought not to be overdone, any more than one would overdo respect for a telephone into which a very distinguished person had spoken.

Lord Quickswood
(directions for his own funeral, remembered by Lord Halifax)

Lord Hugh Cecil − as he was for the first seventy-two years of his life − was the fifth and youngest son of the Prime Minister Lord Salisbury. In his admirable contribution to the Oxford Dictionary of National Biography, *Kenneth Rose tells us that*

although well past the age of forty and never in robust health, Cecil joined the Royal Flying Corps in 1915. His intrepid manoeuvres while learning to fly eventually brought him his pilot's wings − on condition that he never again made a solo flight . . . In 1936 he was appointed Provost of Eton in succession to M.R. James. He delighted in the services in College Chapel and as its ordinary would preface his sermons with the words 'I speak as a layman to laymen without the authority of the priesthood', then go on to be very authoritative indeed. His tall swaying figure surmounted by a green eyeshade, his incisive and often provocative commentary on biblical texts, and his oblique anti-clericalism will all be remembered. So too will his destructive *obiter dicta* on talks to the boys by distinguished visitors. 'I hope I am not boring you,' one of them said nervously in the middle of an address. 'Not yet,' the Provost replied with a tigerish smile.

The distinguished visitor in question was Sir Edwin Lutyens.

(Elizabeth Cavendish wrote: 'My eye lit on the entry on my old Uncle Hugh Cecil which I enjoyed enormously. He used to stay with us very frequently and in the war people would stop this venerable old man in his straw hat and ask him the way to somewhere as all the signposts were removed. His answer was always 'I know the way, but I'm not going to tell you.' He had not the faintest idea of where any of these places were.)

Raymond Chandler wrote in 1948 *to Edward Weeks of* The Atlantic Monthly:

> Would you convey my compliments to the purist who reads your proofs and tell him or her that I write in a sort of broken-down patois, which is something like the way a Swiss waiter talks, and that when I split an infinitive, God damn it, I split it so it will remain split, and when I interrupt the velvety smoothness of my more or less literate syntax with a few sudden words of bar-room vernacular, this is done with the eyes wide open and the mind relaxed but attentive. The method may not be perfect, but it is all I have. I think your proofreader is kindly attempting to steady me on my feet but, much as I appreciate the solicitude, I am really able to steer a pretty clear course, provided I get both sidewalks and the street in between.

From the Obituaries section of the New College Record, 1996:

ROBERT PATRICK (BERTIE) BELL (1960) died at Aix-en-Provence on 30 September 1996 at the age of fifty-four after many brushes with disaster and the loss of all but a few friends. As the son of a war widow, he had been brought up with small expectations, but the care of godparents and the generosity of a grandmother helped him through difficult times. Educated at Marlborough and New College, he read English and was awarded a degree despite the microscopic illegibility of his writing. Here he was confirmed in his love of poetry and a belief in the primacy of pleasure which he never abandoned. Strongly built, pale-skinned and freckled, he had unruly red hair, a leonine grin, a canine cough, and a mischievous glance which disturbed strangers; his manner ensured that he would never lack friends or enemies. Were he charming money from bankers, teasing the philistine, formerly [*sic*] throwing fits and eating banknotes, he made his mark indelible.

After going down he worked for British Petroleum, and British Intelligence, in Tehran, where he acquired a deep contempt for commerce and a Persian wife, Gritty. On his return, the collapse of his marriage and his sanity drove him to teaching, at Padworth College, but an altercation with the Rector, Fison, ended the experiment. In 1968, with the encouragement of David Cecil and under the devoted supervision of Rachel Trickett, he returned to New College as a graduate student. After two years of desultory reading and studious play he was denied a higher degree, although his dissertation on the economics of translation in the later seventeenth century was a minor triumph. His next incarnation, as a London property developer, was precariously financed, and despite the moral support of his second wife, an American, he was obliged to flee his creditors after the crash of 1974, and leave his properties undeveloped. After hiding in Paris, he withdrew to his godmother's house at Uzès, but was tracked down by a London tipstaff and from 1977 to 1984 tried to repay debts by building and refurbishing in the Gard with the help of timely legacies and labour volunteered by local admirers. A brief spell as a lecturer in economics at the *Ecole Nationale d'Administration* ended with an undeserved prosecution for assault, and a series of self-inflicted injuries from which he never fully recovered. Nevertheless, he was able to write: one poem a day, and only in cafés with marble-topped tables. A small selection was published at Nîmes in the journal *L'Ingénu*, as 'Poète et autres légumes'. A few lines reached The Spectator, thanks to Hugh Cecil.*

After he moved to Aix, a serious fall and a surgical error left him toothless and lame, and a further law-suit with a partner brought his business ventures to a halt. In pain and adversity he learned to play the flute, and to earn money thereby in the streets to the west of S. Sauveur. In 1991 he was awarded an 80% disability pension by the state, and retired to a rented room with the intention of learning Chinese and avoiding alcohol. His verses and his music amused a small circle to the end, and he was fortunate in the loyalty of the accomplished chanteuse Catherine Tarrit, and their son Jonathan. His much-abused constitution gave way after a final operation on the oesophagus, and he was buried in the municipal cemetery of Grand S. Jean, where grave-markers are obliterated after five years; an economy of piety after his own heart. Whether his verses will outlast the headstone depends on their being traced and published.

* The writer and critic, not to be confused with the Lord Hugh Cecil, our hero of three pages back.

The article was unsigned; but I have since discovered the author to be Eric Christiansen.

I sent a copy of the Cracker as usual to David Davies, who passed it on to Bell's New College contemporary Alex de Jonge. Mr, de Jonge put his own gloss on the above:

. . . Anglo-Irish, he was truly mad, bad and dangerous to know and had he had a spark of political feeling could easily have been a terrorist like Rose Dugdale.

Shortly after I met him he tried to kill me after finding me having tea with his girl. He drove his mini hard at me and I realised that if I jumped too soon he would swerve, too late and . . . We never mentioned the incident subsequently.

He came back to Oxford to work on a thesis and we played a lot of poker together. He loved stealing pots with large bets, much to the annoyance of Eric, who favoured the fifty p. raise. However on one occasion Eric looked at his hand, took out his note case and very slowly put a fiver on the table. 'We can't have that', said Bell, who put the note in his mouth and swallowed it, slowly, with the aid of several gulps of whisky while Eric looked sadly on . . .

He gave up on his thesis and went in for property speculation . . . Soon after he went to Teheran to teach English and married a Persian girl in an Islamic ceremony having adopted the faith. Since the only language they had in common was Russian, which they both spoke execrably, the marriage did not last. On his return he spent a fortune in legal fees in an attempt to get divorced, only to have counsel finally opine that he had not been married in the first place.

Whether in music or architecture, literature, painting or sculpture, art opens our eyes, ears and feelings to something beyond ourselves, something we cannot experience without the artist's vision and the genius of his craft. The placing of Greek temples, like the Temple of Poseidon on the promontory at Sunion, outlined against the piercing blue of the Aegean Sea, Poseidon's home; the majesty of Michelangelo's sculptured figures in stone; Shakespeare's command of language and knowledge of the human soul; the intricate order of Bach, the enchantment of Mozart; the purity of Chinese monochrome pottery with its lovely names – celadon, oxblood, peach blossom, clair de lune; the exuberance of Tiepolo's ceilings where, without picture frames to limit movement, a whole world in exquisitely beautiful colors lives and moves in the sky; the prose and poetry of all the writers from Homer to Cervantes to Jane Austen and John Keats to Dostoevsky and Chekhov – who made all these things? We – our species – did. The range is too vast and various to do justice to it in this space, but the random samples I have mentioned, and all the rest they suggest, are sufficient reason to honor mankind.

Barbara Tuchman
Practising History

The following letter – of which I possess a photocopy and which I quote in its entirety – was addressed by the 5th Baron Rayleigh to the Marquess of Hertford. It was unsolicited.

Terling Place
Chemsford
Essex

19 May 1987

Dear Lord Hertford,
I proclaimed myself King on the death of King George VI.
I had no idea of the trouble into which this action would lead me.
Yours sincerely,
Rayleigh

The Muséum Histoire Naturelle [sic] of La Rochelle contains a stuffed giraffe, known as 'La Girafe de Charles X'. In an accompanying inscription, the animal tells its own story:

Mon histoire relève de la diplomatie du début du XIXème. Le Pacha d'Egypte Méhémet-Ali, voulant amadouer en 1825 le Roi de France, décide sur les conseils de Bernadino Drovetti, consul de France, d'offrir un exemplaire de mon espèce au souverain Charles X. Premier problème: le consul d'Angleterre est jaloux; heureusement nous sommes deux girafeaux tout juste arrivés du Soudan, on tire au sort, le plus robuste (moi) échoit au Roi de France. Deuxième problème: le voyage! Drovetti organise tout, un bateau sarde légèrement modifié, un palefrenier égyptien, trois domestiques soudanais et trois vaches pour me fournir les 25 litres de lait quotidien et nous quittons Alexandrie. Le 23 octobre 1826, nous arrivons à Marseille: émoi dans le pays: jamais une girafe vivante n'est arrivée en France! Je loge à la préfecture, entourée de soins et d'affection même, par les Villeneuve-Bargemont! L'hiver terminé, ces messieurs du Muséum décident de me faire prendre le chemin de Paris, évidemment à pied et avec un imperméable de toile pour le mauvais temps! 20 mai-30 juin: en fait, promenade merveilleuse de Marseille à Paris, avec une foule d'admirateurs déchaînés! Début juillet, rencontre avec le souverain, il est très impressioné! Pour moi c'est le début d'un séjour qui allait durer 17 ans et demi à la ménagerie du Jardin des Plantes. En 1845 je trépassai, fus naturalisée et pris place dans la galerie de zoologie du Muséum avant d'être donnée, grâce au Professeur Bourdelle, en 1931, au Muséum de la Rochelle.

My story begins with early 19th-century diplomacy. Mehmet Ali, Pasha of Egypt, anxious in 1825 to appease the King of France, decides on the advice of the French Consul, Bernadino Drovetti, to send an example of my species to the sovereign, Charles X. Problem No. 1: the English Consul is jealous; fortunately there are two of us young giraffes just arrived from the Sudan. Lots are drawn, and I (the stronger of the two) fall

to the King of France. Problem No. 2: the journey! Drovetti
arranges everything – a Sardinian ship (slightly modified),
an Egyptian groom, three Sudanese servants and three cows
to provide me with my 25 litres of milk a day – and so we
leave Alexandria. On 23 October 1826 we arrive at Marseille.
Excitement throughout the country: never before has a living
giraffe set foot in France! I am put up at the Prefecture, the
Villeneuve-Bargemont family showering me with little favours
and even affection! Winter past, the gentlemen of the Museum
decide that I should take the road to Paris, naturally on foot
and with a canvas waterproof for bad weather! 20 May – 30
June: a wonderful walk indeed, from Marseille to Paris, with
crowds of vociferous admirers! At the beginning of July I meet
the monarch: he is deeply impressed! For me this is the start of a
seventeen-and-a-half-year stay in the menagerie of the Jardin des
Plantes. I died in 1845, was duly stuffed and took my place in
the Zoological Gallery of the Museum before being presented,
thanks to Professor Bourdelle, to the Museum of La Rochelle.'

The One remains, the many change and pass;
Heaven's light forever shines, Earth's shadows fly;
Life, like a dome of many-coloured glass,
Stains the white radiance of Eternity,
Until Death tramples it to fragments.

Shelley, *Adonais*

BONUS

Venice, as well as giving birth to one of the most dazzling schools of painting the world has ever seen, has also inspired much fine writing – though more often by foreigners than by native Venetians or even Italians. Occasionally, however, she becomes the victim of descriptions so atrocious as to boast a certain monstrous grandeur of their own. Here is the worst I know, an article commissioned by the Alitalia in-flight magazine from a certain Germano Lombardi:

Venice, a friend curled up in the violet eye of the dolphin formed by the Mediterranean. The dolphin's image, so a legend from Byzantium says, is inscribed in the golden book which the winged lion of St Mark, rearing on a column by the lagoon, holds in his solemn paws. Venice, a space of sand and earth, of water and humble, sparse vegetation, of reed and rush forests tormented by destiny and the years. In Venice, the symbols of animals cross their tracks, eternally nodding at far-off times.

There, these symbols, which also represent mythical figures like the dragon and the phoenix, have been fixed in the minds of the world's peoples by thousands of books, musical compositions, statues, pictures, churches, palaces, and monuments. In Venice, even the pig's greedy snort has become an ideogram and a symbol, for both wile and religious faith. According to tradition, the mortal remains of St Mark, the city's guardian saint, were hidden in the belly of a slaughtered pig by skilful merchants trading in Moslem lands. For the Moslem customs officers at the port of Cairo [*sic*], the pig was an impure animal. They felt such repugnance for the impious carrion that they failed to make a proper search and let the heathen Venetians continue on their way. Blown by a favourable wind, they took three days and seven hours to bear the saint's remains to that spot in front of the Doge's Palace where there now stands the lofty column topped by the winged, roaring lion.

If you happened to be at the column's foot on the morning of March 24, 1978, you would have had the privilege of meeting the rose-coloured grace of Joan Fleur Springtime, nineteen years old, from Boston (Mass.) Joan admired the rutless waters of the lagoon. A list of passage ways, places and alleys will tell her how to find the painted images of a love born at Selene in Libya between St George, a Venetian, and a young Arab princess. At this time, George looked like an American actor named Robert Redford. The princess resembles nothing more or less than fleeting, feminine grace. It was then that the great master of the Dalmatian and Slav school, Carpaccio, saw her, standing somewhat perplexed and something of a snob before the dragon which George would then slay with such sang-froid.

The picture hangs in San Giovanni del Tempio, a Venetian church like a calm, discreet, secluded London club. But, if you are patient and continue towards St Mark's Square, right beside the bell-tower when the weather is good, you will usually find Signor Arcain, who has the most subtle information about his city. For example, certain words and expressions in the Venetian dialect, which is a language, a resonant, extravagant, and living language. Motionless at Signor Arcain's side as he speaks is a glorious mongrel. Further ahead, the musicians playing in the cafés, the pigeons, and an affectionate fool who has been driven crazy by the beauty of such a free and rectangular space.

A jet overhead beyond the gilded cupolas, the marble and the violet-coloured thoughts that come to anyone walking on the echoing paving-stones. Off to one side, the bell tower like a sundial's indexfinger, its shadow following the time, the weather and the seasons from dawn to sunset, following the clouds, and something which is not for sale, but is there.

Not on sale, because it cannot be bought, because it is as incommunicable as *The Tempest* by Giorgione, one of the local artists – a painting that anyone can see at the Academy. So look at the bell tower without renouncing a look at *The Tempest*! Then, calmly turn your back and walk towards the great portico at the other end of the square. Half-way there, if you have sensitive nostrils, you will smell the subtle scent of a drink, that small, ice-cold mixture served in a chalice-shaped glass and known the world over as a Martini. Follow the scent and, thirty-eight paces after the portico, turn into the alleyway on your right. Another twenty-seven steps, and there on the right, you will find the world's most famous bar: Harry's Bar, whose birth has been recounted by the man who both fathered and mothered it, Signor Cipriani. In the well-lighted room, you can hear the dancing of useless, gay chatter in a thousand tongues. Laughter, the nod of heads, and the light happiness of holiday time. Outside, a gondolier shouting '*Ohé!*', the ferries, and the restless movement of the Great Canal, a liquid promenade so extraordinary that you almost feel an ache, especially when a wise old man beside you looks at Venice, his friend, and remarks, 'Beauty is hope's apparel!'

Beyond the Grand Canal, there is the point with the church of Santa Maria della Salute. The gilded sphere topping this St Mary of Good Health seems proud of an ancient well-being. It does not glitter just in the sun, but also in the air, wind and humid landscape of the 'Serenissima'. Under that glittering sphere, the affectionate and ironic eye of Gastone Novelli, the painter, saw the passage of Chinese ships cloaked in a red-silken summons and fluttering with world revolution.

Continue, dear lady, at a slow pace! Your gentle body will become as light as a kite, and the memory of ancient happiness will walk with you laughing. Beyond the promontory of S. Maria della Salute, the Giudecca Canal and the island of S. Giorgio Maggiore, where you can see 1000 greedy seagulls, 55 motorboats and a single gondola which, if you're romantic, seems laden with a cargo of pain. So, cross the bridge and walk the alleys! Climb the bell towers, enter the quiet shade of the 27 churches, 18 museums, and 300 hostelries jubilant with voices. Try to pick out the numberless smells, scents and stinks which, depending on the time and season, hove over the city. Pick out the noises of the night, the pauses of silence between them, the violet trapezes of light which reach as far as the constellation of Andromeda, on wintry nights when the freezing *bora* blows, and you crouch down at the Hotel Danieli, in the world's most comfortable beds, sleeping and dreaming of great moons as red as a strawberry omelette. There are cats on the roofs, looking for somewhere warm, by a chimney with a view to the East.

In St Stephen's Square, there is a child nicknamed 'Nous' with a limping gull on a lead. On the Rialto Bridge, a drunk gazes at the Canal. With pensive eyes, he says, 'I'm almost six feet tall, I weigh 150 pounds . . . so I'm perfection and beauty personified . . .'

A Christmas Cracker

2004

What song the Syrens sang, or what name Achilles assumed when he hid himself among women, though puzzling questions, are not beyond all conjecture.

Sir Thomas Browne
Urn Burial

(My friend John Parker writes that he is mystified: is not the song of the Syrens accurately recorded in the Odyssey, Book XII, lines 184-190?

Robert Dagles translates the lines:

'Come closer, famous Odysseus – Achaea's pride and glory! –
Moor your ship on our coast so you can hear our song!
Never has any sailor passed our shores in his black craft
Until he has heard the honeyed voices pouring from our lips,
And once he hears to his heart's content sails on, a wise man;
We know all the pains that the Greeks and Trojans once endured
Or the spreading plains of Troy when the gods willed it so –
al that comes to pass onk the futile earth, we know it all!'

The answer to John's question is, therefore, up to a point, but they are only inviting him to listen: their invitation is only a trailer to the song itself. Odysseus, roped to his mast, never gets to hear the full programme.)

Hernando de Soto was Spanish,
An iron-clad conquistador.
Adventures he knew in the sack of Peru
But it just made him anxious for more.

Hernando de Soto was knightly,
Hernando de Soto was bold,
But like most of his lot he'd be off like shot
Wherever he heard there was gold.

So with priest and physician and army,
Not to speak of a number of swine,
At Tampa he started a quest, fiery-hearted,
For the gold of a fabulous mine.

And from Florida way out to Texas,
This Don of a single-track mind
Went chasing his dream over prairie and stream
And the pigs went on trotting behind.

He discovered the great Mississippi,
Faced perils and hardships untold,
And his soldiers ate bacon, if I'm not mistaken,
But nobody found any gold.

They buried de Soto at midnight
Where the wide Mississippi still jigs;
He was greedy for gain, but a soldier of Spain.
(I hope someone looked after the pigs.)

Rosemary and Stephen Vincent Benét

It is commonly said that hope goes with youth, and lends to youth its wings of a butterfly: but I fancy that hope is the last gift given to man, and the only gift not given to youth. Youth is pre-eminently the period in which a man can be lyric, fanatical, poetic; but youth is a period in which a man can be hopeless. The end of every episode is the End of the World. But the power of hoping through everything, the knowledge that the soul survives its adventures, this great inspiration comes to the middle-aged; God has kept this good wine until now. It is from the backs of the elderly gentlemen that the wings of the butterfly should burst. There is nothing that so much mystifies the young as the constant frivolity of the old. They have discovered their indestructibility. They are in their second and clearer childhood, and there is a meaning in the merriment of their eyes. They have seen the end of the End of the World.

G.K. Chesterton

On 23 January 2004 I attended the funeral of my life-long friend Raymond Bonham Carter at Stockton, Wiltshire. When it was over the congregation was most kindly invited by Mr and Mrs Nicholas Yeatman-Biggs to tea and drinks in their beautiful house opposite the church. Wakes of this kind, in my experience, are nearly always happy occasions; I like to think of the deceased seeing all his or her old friends gathered together enjoying themselves. But on this particular occasion there was an unexpected bonus: in the downstairs loo hung an extract from the journal of the 11th Hussars – the translation of an article in a French newspaper about King George V fishing.

King George V is an angler of the first order, this King of Britain. Behold him there, as he sits motionless under his umbrella, patiently regarding his many-coloured floats. How obstinately he contends with the elements. It is a summer day of Britain – that is to say a day of sleet and fog and tempest. But what would you, it is as they love it, those who follow the sport.

Presently the King's float begins to descend – My God! but how he strikes! The hook is implanted in the very bowels of the salmon. The King rises – he spurns aside his footstool – he strides strongly and swiftly towards the rear.

In due course the salmon comes to approach himself to the bank. Aha! The King has cast aside his rod – he hurls himself flat on the ground on his victim – they splash and struggle in the icy water. But it is a braw Laddie the Gillie, a kind of outdoor domestic, administers the *coup de grâce* with his pistol. The King cries with a shrill voice 'Hip, Hip, Hoorah!'

On this red-letter day His Majesty King George V dines on a haggis and whisky grog. Like a true Scotsman he wears only a kilt.

More dictionary definitions sent to me by my pen-friend David Langford, this time from MacAlpine's Gaelic Dictionary, *1833*:

Brochanach:	Well supplied with porridge
Dobharchu:	An imaginary otter
Rotach:	A circle of filth on one's clothes
Paitireachd:	Phrenology, thumping
Sgiomlaireachd:	Mean habit of popping in upon people at mealtimes
Sginnach:	A charm or enchantment to enable its possessor to get all the fish around a boat or headland while his less fortunate neighbours stare with amazement
Spairis:	The conduct or attitude of having the hands in the flaps of the trousers

Autumn and winter are best for walking. There is a bite in the air that lifts the foot easily, under the wayward last warmth of the sun. When that, too, goes, and the rims of dead leaves lie rigid with frost across the stiffened ruts of the road, another pleasure is added: for the earth, no longer hidden in her softness, answers with a dim echo, a muffled thud, to every step; so that on a hard road one can play a game clapped in time on the surface of the planet, with astonishment that an object so big and unmanageable as the world rings back to a human foot.

The pleasure of travel is in this answer of the whole earth, potentially, to our steps, so that every good journey must have in it some measure of exploration, and, if possible, an effort of our own. There is no need to go far; a John Gilpin day is enough: imagination only is needed – and an awareness of the horizon rim beyond which the world is new. And if one were asked which, of all the sights in nature, is most lastingly satisfying, would one not choose the horizon?

Freya Stark
Perseus in the Wind

On 19 June 1891, Robert Louis Stevenson sent to Henry Clay Ide, American Land Commissioner in Samoa, the following declaration:

I, Robert Louis Stevenson, Advocate of the Scots Bar, author of *The Master of Ballantrae* and *Moral Emblems,* stuck civil engineer, sole owner and patentee of the Palace and Plantation known as Vailima in the island of Upolu, Samoa, a British Subject, being in sound mind and pretty well I thank you in body:

In consideration that Miss A.H. Ide, daughter of H.C. Ide, in the town of St Johnsbury, in the County of Caledonia, in the State of Vermont, United States of America, was born, out of all reason, upon Christmas Day, and is therefore, out of all justice, denied the consolation and profit of a Proper Birthday:

And considering that I, the said Robert Louis Stevenson, have attained an age when O , we never mention it[1] and that I have now no further use for a birthday of any description:

And in consideration that I have met H.C. Ide, the father of the said A.H. Ide, and found him about as white a Land Commissioner as I require:

Have transferred and *do hereby transfer* to the said A.H. Ide, *All and Whole* my rights and privileges in the thirteenth day of November, formerly my birthday, new, hereby, and henceforth, the birthday of the said A.H. Ide, to have, hold, exercise and enjoy the same in the customary manner, by the sporting of fine raiment, eating of rich meats and receipt of gifts, compliments and copies of verse, according to the manner of our ancestors;

And I direct the said A.H. Ide to add to her said name of A.H. Ide the name of Louisa – at least in private; and I charge her to use my said birthday with moderation and humanity, *et tamquam bona filia familiae,* the said birthday not being so young as it once was and having carried me in a very satisfactory manner since I can remember;

And in case the said A.H. Ide shall neglect or contravene either of the above conditions, I hereby revoke the donation and transfer my rights in the said birthday to the President of the United States of America for the time being:

In witness whereof I have hereto set my hand and seal this nineteenth day of June in the year of grace eighteen hundred and ninety-one.

Witness: Lloyd Osbourne
Witness: Harold Watts

Robert Louis Stevenson
I.P.D.[2]

President Theodore Roosevelt is said to have checked up.

[1]"There was a popular song at time called *Oh no, we never mention her,* by Thomas Haynes Bayley.

[2]*In praesentia dominorum* – In presence of the Lords (of Session). Under Scottish law these letters are added to the signature of the presiding judge in the Court of Session to indicate that he has signed in the presence of the other judges.

In China letters are respected not merely to a degree but in a sense which must seem, I think, to you unintelligible and overstrained. But there is a reason for it. Our poets and literary men have taught their successors, for long generations, to look for good not in wealth, not in power, not in miscellaneous activity, but in a trained, a choice, an exquisite appreciation of the most simple and universal relations of life. To feel, and in order to feel to express, or at least to understand the expression of all that is lovely in Nature, of all that is poignant and sensitive in man, is to us in itself a sufficient end. A rose in a moonlit garden, the shadow of trees on the turf, almond bloom, scent of pine, the wine-cup and the guitar; these and the pathos of life and death, the long embrace, the hand stretched out in vain, the moment that glides for ever away, with its freight of music and light, into the shadow and hush of the haunted past, all that we have, all that eludes us, a bird on the wing, a perfume escaped on the gale – to all these things we are trained to respond, and the response is what we call literature.

G. Lowes Dickinson
Letters from a Chinese Official

*My dear son Jason has thoughtfully provided me with the following
list of condom flavours currently available on platform 1 of the railway
station in Lady Thatcher's home town of Grantham, Lincolnshire:*

Strawberries and Cream
Ice Cream
Lemon and Lime
Banana
Liquorice
Champagne
Whisky
Curry
Lager
Chocdoms
Humpy Birthday
Tropical Nights
Lads' Night Out
Kangaroo

Outside of a dog, a book is man's best friend. Inside of a dog,
it's too dark to read.

Groucho Marx

*(Writing in August 2009, I am delighted to see that that admirable
man of letters Rick Gekoski has just published a book entitled*
Outside of a Dog. *I bought it entirely for the title – and I am very
glad I did.)*

Thomas Hearne (1678-1735) was an entertaining eccentric who was Assistant Keeper of the Bodleian Library in Oxford, and would have been Keeper had he been prepared to take the oath of loyalty to the House of Hanover. This, however, he regarded as being a usurping dynasty, and preferred (as he put it) 'a good conscience before all manner of preferment and worldly honour'. In his Reliquiae Bodleianae *he writes the following, under the date of 3 June 1706:*

In the Bodlejan library, among the MSS in Mus. num. 235 [now 242] are the Epistles of St Paul &c, printed in an old black letter, in 12mo., which was queen Elizabeth's own book, and her hand writing appears at the beginning, viz.

August.

I walke many times into the pleasant fieldes of the holy scriptures, where I plucke up the goodliesome herbes of sentences by pruning: eate them by reading: chewe them up by musing: and laie them up at length in the hie seate of memorie, by gathering them together: that so having tasted the sweetenes, I may the lesse perceave the bitternes of this miserable life.

From a letter of Martyn Skinner – the son of Sir Sydney Skinner, Chairman of Barker's – to R.C. Hutchinson, March 1963:

. . . You will, I hope, be calling in here in a fortnight and I must give you directions. Well, you come to Taunton – or Tarnton as we have to call it – and then take the A3 something to Bampton, through Newton Fitzwarren and past the Bath and West Showground, and a village I ominously misread as Hellcomin' (we were nearly killed at Newt Fitz in January – black ice), well, then you come to Preston Bowyer, all on A3 whatever it is, and then – suddenly – on the brow of a hill, a most difficult turn (but you have to make it) a turning to Fitzhead. Take it. It will lead to Fitzhead – if you don't turn off to Halse or Milverton. Reaching Fitzhead you will see an imposing wall with buttresses which (according to the owner) was mentioned in Doomsday Book – well, you should have turned *left* before reaching the wall, so you'll have to turn round and come back and now turn right, which will bring you past the church. Here you will see the Council estate – ignore it (if you can) also a house of Swedish construction with blue windows. (Notice, however, the begging notice by the church to say the church is falling down, which is falling down itself.) Well, then you will see a house with tall chimnies (some of them dummies) which ought to be called *Tall Chimnies* but isn't – this is Ilex House – this is us. You can't miss it.

From *Two Men of Letters, Correspondence 1957-74*
ed. *Rupert Hart-Davis*

And talking of chimneys – as I prefer to spell them – how about this passage, from my friend Peter Vansittart's dazzling book In Memory of England?

The chimneys of the Great Houses – coiffed and knobbed, hooded, ruffed, coned, ledged, rimmed, pargeted or plain, patterned in diamond, lozenge, criss-cross, bristling with decorative unnecessaries: chimneys squat as petards, narrow as cannons trained on the noon sun, bulging like midget volcanoes: chimneys like a zed or Roman I: like tubs, stove-pipe hats, like judges, jurymen, brooding monks: chimneys ochred, black, slate-grey, blood-red: a jungle of shapes, at dusk becoming giant inert frogs, mitres, witches' hats, dim candytwists, cowled shoulders, smudged pinnacles, tops of pagodas, even concertinas, symbols of this, reminders of that, an effort towards poetry – still fret the skyline, for pause and rumination.

She poured tea. The oil-lamps cast a warm light on the tea-tray. The teapot was china, with little roses painted all over it, crimson and blush-pink and celestial blue, and the cups were garlanded with the same flowers. There were sugared biscuits, each with a flower made out of piped icing, creamy, violet, snow-white. Sophy Sheekhy watched the stream of topaz-coloured liquid fall from the spout, steaming and aromatic. This too was a miracle, that gold-skinned persons in China and bronze-skinned persons in India should gather leaves which should come across the seas safely in white-winged ships, encased in lead, encased in wood, surviving storms and whirlwinds, sailing on under hot sun and cold moon, and come here, and be poured from bone-china, made from fine clay, moulded by clever fingers, in the Pottery Towns, baked in kilns, glazed with slippery shiny clay, baked again, painted with rosebuds by artist-hands holding fine, fine brushes, delicately turning the potter's wheel and implanting, with a kiss of sable-hairs, floating buds on an azure ground, or a dead white ground, and that sugar should be fetched from where black men and women slaved and died terribly to make these delicate flowers that melted on the tongue like the scrolls in the mouth of the Prophet Isaiah, that flour should be milled, and milk shaken into butter, and both worked together into these momentary delights, baked in Mrs Jesse's oven and piled elegantly on to a plate to be offered to Captain Jesse with his wool-white head and smiling eyes, to Mrs Papagay, flushed and agitated, to her sick self, and the black bird and the dribbling Pug, in front of the hot coals of fire, in the benign lamplight. Any of them might so easily not have been there, to drink the tea, or eat the sweetmeats. Storms and ice-floes might have taken Captain Jesse, grief or childbearing might have destroyed his wife, Mrs Papagay might have lapsed into penury and she herself have died as an overworked servant, but here they were and their eyes were bright and their tongues tasted goodness.

A.S. Byatt
The Conjugal Angel
(from *Angels and Insects*)

Prayer

Prayer the Churches banquet, Angels age,
   God's breath in man returning to his birth,
   The soul in paraphrase, heart in pilgrimage,
The Christian plummet sounding heav'n and earth;
Engine against th' Almightie, sinners towre,
   Reversed thunder, Christ-side-piercing spear,
   The six-daies world transposing in an houre,
A kind of tune, which all things heare and fear;

Softnesse, and peace, and joy, and love, and blisse,
   Exalted Manna, gladnesse of the best,
   Heaven in ordinarie, man well drest,
The milkie way, the bird of Paradise,
   Church-bells beyond the starres heard, the souls bloud,
   The land of spices; something understood.

George Herbert

I have no very clear idea of what this means, but if it isn't poetry I don't know what is.

The following is extracted from an interview with Madonna by the Hungarian magazine Blikk. *The questions were asked in Hungarian and then translated into English. Madonna's replies were then translated into Hungarian. The interview was then published in Hungarian, and finally translated back into English.* Time Magazine *commented that 'to say that something was lost in the process is to be wildly ungrateful for all that was gained'.*

Blikk: Madonna, Budapest says hello with arms that are spread-eagled. Are you in good odor? You are the biggest fan of our young people who hear your musical productions and like to move their bodies in response.

Madonna: (Holds up hands) Please stop with taking sensationalist photographs until I have removed my garments for all to see. *(Laughs)* That is a joke I have made.

Blikk: Madonna, let's cut to toward the hunt. Are you a bold hussy-woman that feasts on men who are tops?

Madonna: Yes, yes, this is certainly something that brings to the surface my longings. In America it is not considered to be mentally ill when a woman advances on her prey in a discotheque setting with hardy cocktails present. And there is a more normal attitude toward leather play-toys that also makes my day.

Blikk: Is this how you met Carlos, your love-servant who is reputed? Did you know he was heaven-sent right off the stick? Or were you dating many others in your bed at the same time?

Madonna: No, he was the only one I was dating in my bed then, so it is a scientific fact that the baby was made in my womb using him. But I am a woman and not a test-mouse! Carlos is an everyday person in the orbit of a star who is being muscle-trained by him not a sex machine.

Blikk: May we talk about your other 'baby', your movie, then? Please do not be denying that the similarities between you and the real Evita are grounded in basis. Power, money, tasty-food, Grammys – all these elements are afoot.

Madonna: What is up in the air with you? Evita never was winning a Grammy!

Blikk: Perhaps not. But as to your film, in trying to bring your reputation along a rocky road, can you make people forget the bad explosions of Who's That Girl? And Shanghai Surprise?

Madonna: I am a tip-top starlet. That is the job I am paid to do.

Blikk: OK, here's a question from left space. What was your book Slut about?

Madonna: It was called Sex, my book.

Blikk: Here it was called Slut. How did it come to publish? Were you lovemaking with a man-about-town printer? Do you prefer making suggestive literature to fast selling CDs?

Madonna: These are different facets to my career highway. I am preferring only to become respected all over the map as a 100% artist.

Blikk: How many Hungarian men have you dated in bed? Are they No. 1? How are they comparing to Argentine men, who are famous for being tip-top as well?

Madonna: Well, to avoid aggravating global tension, I won't say. It's a tie. *(Laughs)* No no, I am serious now. See here, I am working like a canine all the way around the clock!

Blikk: Thank you for your candid chitchat.

Madonna: No problem, friend who is a girl.

They said that it could not be done:
With a laugh he went right to it.
He tackled the thing that couldn't be done –
And couldn't do it.

Anon.

After which one can only hope that he remembered that great maxim of Ogden Nash:

If at first you don't succeed, the hell with it.

Tennyson and Henry James are the source of more good anecdotes than any other English writer. We had some of Tennyson's in 2001; now it's James's turn. Several fine examples occur in A.C. Benson's letters to Geoffrey Madan. Here, for example, is James on the conversation of Mark Twain:

'He thought, he thought, in fact he seemed to think, he seemed to claim, in a word he *claimed* that all the time at *our* disposal was at *his* disposal.' Then H.J. went on to say that Mark Twain seemed to be thinking aloud: 'He retracted, he emphasized, he withdrew his emphasis, he corrected in public, he revised, he modified the scheme of his sentence, he filched away an adjective, he dabbed on a word . . . it was inconceivable, indecent, pathological!'

In another letter Benson writes:

I had a busy day in town – but having to wait for my lawyer – my appointment being at 3 and he being engaged with other clients – I gave him mentally till 3.15 and then simply went away without a word . . . When after this bout I returned to my club, there was Henry James going away in a cab. We shook hands – he said he was going to catch a train, and I had an appointment in a few minutes. He said to me that I looked adventurous. I told him about my flight from my lawyer. He said 'Well my dear Arthur, I feel that I can't, at this cloudy and hurried moment, do *justice* to your anecdote. But I will take it with me, I will *reflect* upon it – yes, I will certainly *reflect* – and you may assuredly count on my discovering something to your advantage in it.' He then gave me a sort of benediction – and it is difficult to receive one in the right frame of mind when you feel pretty sure it is going to make you miss your appointment, and quite certain it is going to lose the beatificer his train.

Finally:

I lunched with Henry James, who was immensely pontifical. He spoke of Edmund Gosse, and his inability to make friends or keep them. Then he said: 'Yet the worst of it is, that in some cloudy corner of that shallow mind, a ghastly conception of possible intimacy seems to lurk.' He said that Gosse had written to him to say that he (G.) was much vexed never to receive a signal of interest from H.J. and that all the advances had to be made by him (G.), but adding that he nevertheless would ask him to dine &c. H.J. held up his hands in horror and added: 'With what hope of arousing an emotion, or in quest of *what* emotion, I can scarcely divine! What preface could be more skilfully adapted to destroy every species of pleasurable anticipation, every prompting of memory and affection?'

But Gosse could certainly put the boot in when he wanted to. Here he is on Sir William Davenant:

There is not a more hopelessly faded laurel on the slopes of the English Parnassus than that which once flourished so bravely around the grotesque head of Davenant. The enormous folio edition of his works, brought out in 1673 in direct emulation of Ben Jonson, is probably the most deplorable collection of verses anywhere to be found, dead and dusty beyond the wont of forgotten classics. The critic is inclined to say that everything is spurious about Davenant, from the legend that connects his blood with Shakespeare's to the dramatic genius that his latest contemporaries praised so highly. He is not merely a ponderous, he is a nonsensical writer, and having begun life by writing meaningless romantic plays in imitation of Massinger, and insipid masques in the school of Ben Jonson, he closed his long and busy career by parodying the style of Dryden. But he really deserves to be classed with none of these authors, but with Sir William Killigrew and Sir Robert Stapleton, the dullest crew of pedants and poetasters which our literature has seen. From this wide condemnation of the writings of Davenant, his romantic epic of *Gondibert* must be excepted. It is a poem of chivalry the scene of which is laid in Lombardy, but of which the author grew tired before it had occurred to him to construct a plot. It is, accordingly, nothing but an incoherent, rambling fragment, through which the reader toils, as if through a quicksand, dragging his steps along, and rewarded every now and then by a firmer passage containing some propriety of thought or a beautiful single line.

In the 1983 Cracker I quoted what I thought was a rather lovely song of Davenant's, mentioning that I knew two interesting things about him. First, he liked to think that he was the illegitimate son of Shakespeare – which he may well have been, since his father kept the Crown Inn at Oxford, where the Bard always put up on his journeys between Stratford and London. Second, he had no nose; as John Aubrey explains, 'He gott a terrible clap of a Black handsome wench that lay in Axe-yard, Westminster . . . which cost him his Nose, with which unlucky mischance many witts were cruelly bold.'

Before, however, the moon had glided more than a soundless pace or two on her night journey, Myfanwy and her incomparable ass were safely out of sight.

Walter de la Mare
The Lovely Myfanwy, 1925

From the lone shieling of the misty island
  Mountains divide us, and the waste of seas –
Yet still the blood is strong, the heart is Highland,
  And we in dreams behold the Hebrides.

'Canadian Boat Song'

These wonderful lines, and the rest of the poem of which they form the second verse, are one of the unsolved mysteries of literature.

They first appeared, as far as I know, in September 1829 in Blackwood's Magazine, *where they were reported as being a translation from the Gaelic. But if so, who translated them? The poem – or the translation – has been attributed to at least half a dozen different writers, including Sir Walter Scott, James Hogg, John Gibson Lockhart, John Gait, Professor John Wilson of Edinburgh ('Christopher North') and even the 12th Earl of Eglinton. The first edition of the* Oxford Dictionary of Quotations *tentatively suggests Scott, the fourth plumps for Gait: we can take our choice.*

And why 'Canadian'? In the Times Literary Supplement *of 23 December 1904 – exactly a hundred years ago – a Mr G.M. Fraser quotes a letter telling of how its writer 'was lately rowed down the St Lawrence, for several days on end, by a set of strapping fellows, all born in that country, and yet hardly any of whom could speak a word of any tongue but Gaelic. They sung [sic] heaps of our old Highland oar-songs capitally well, in the true Hebridean fashion.' This poem, in its original, was presumably one of them.*

King William IV, who reigned from 1830 to 1837, was my great-great-great-great-grandfather, through one of the copious brood that he fathered on Dorothy Jordan, the leading musical-comedy actress of her day. He succeeded his elder brother George IV on 26 June 1830. On 16 July Charles Greville wrote in his diary:

Never was an elevation like that of King William IV. His life has been hitherto passed in obscurity and neglect, in miserable poverty, surrounded by a numerous progeny of bastards, without consideration or friends, and he was ridiculous for his grotesque ways and little meddling curiosity. Nobody ever invited him into their house, or thought it necessary to honour him with any mark of attention or respect; and so he went on for above forty years, till Canning brought him into notice by making him Lord High Admiral at the time of his grand Ministerial schism. In that post he distinguished himself by making ridiculous speeches, by a morbid official activity, and by a general wildness which was thought to indicate incipient insanity, till shortly after Canning's death and the Duke of Wellington's accession, as is well known, the latter dismissed him.

As King, William in fact arguably proved to be an improvement on his predecessor. Socially, however, he remained something of a liability. His biographer Philip Ziegler notes that 'his vast repertoire of dirty stories made him the terror of every genteel drawing-room.' Here is Greville again, writing on 17 September 1831:

The talk of the town has been about the King and a toast he gave at a great dinner at St James's the other day. He had ninety guests – all his Ministers, all the great people, and all the foreign Ambassadors. After dinner he made a long, rambling, speech in French, and ended by giving as 'a sentiment'*, as he called it, 'The land we live in'. This was before the ladies left the room. After they were gone he made another speech also in French, in the course of which he travelled over every variety of topic that suggested itself to his excursive mind, and ended thus: *'Je vous ai déjà donné un sentiment, et à présent je vais vous en donner un autre. Je vous donnerai donc 'les yeux qui tuent, les fesses qui remuent, et le cul qui danse, honi soit qui mal y pense.'* Sefton, who told it me, said he never felt so ashamed; Lord Grey was ready to sink into the earth; everybody laughed of course, and Sefton, who sat next to Talleyrand, said to him, *'Eh bien, que pensez-vous de cela ?'* With his unmoved, immovable face he answered only, *'C'est bien remarquable.'*

('I have already given you one sentiment, and now I'll give you another: 'The eyes that kill, the thighs that wriggle and the arse that dances. Evil be to him that evil thinks.'*)

Valentine

My heart has made its mind up
And I'm afraid it's you.
Whatever you've got lined up,
My heart has made its mind up,
And if you can't be signed up
This year, next year will do.
My heart has made its mind up
And I'm afraid it's you.

Wendy Cope

As you grow old, you lose interest in sex, your friends drift away, your children often ignore you. There are many other advantages of course, but these would seem to me to be the outstanding ones.

Richard Nerdham
Toronto Globe and Mail

BONUS

Many years ago – I think it was in 1981 or thereabouts – I was invited by the Royal Liverpool Philharmonic Society to do some Christmas readings to accompany the music at the Society's annual Carol Service. They asked me to prepare nine separate readings; going through them in the train, however, I realised that one of them was simply not up to snuff. I had long ago reflected on the honour of being the recipient of the world's most famous Christmas list, so then and there – on the back of an envelope as it were – I wrote a dozen short thankyou letters. They seemed to go down rather well; a few years later they were published separately, with delightful illustrations by Quentin Blake. I never put them in a Cracker at the time, because they were too long for a page; but I think they may do quite nicely as a bonus here.

25 December:

My dearest darling – that partridge, in that lovely little pear tree! What an enchanting, poetic, romantic present! Bless you and thank you. Your deeply loving Emily.

26 December:

My beloved Edward – two turtle – doves arrived this morning and are cooing away in the pear tree as I write. I'm so touched, and grateful. With undying love, as always, Emily.

27 December:

My darling Edward – you do think up the most original presents; whoever thought of sending anyone *hens* – and French ones at that?

Do they really come all the way from France? Unfortunately we have no hen – coops, but I expect we'll manage. Thank you anyway, they're lovely. Your loving Emily.

28 December:

Dearest Edward – What a surprise! Four calling birds arrived this morning. They're very sweet, even if they do call rather loudly; they make telephoning awfully difficult. But they'll probably calm down when they get used to their new home. Anyway I'm very grateful – of course I am. Love from Emily.

29 December:

Dearest Edward – the postman has just delivered five most beautiful gold rings, one for each finger and all fitting perfectly. A really lovely present – lovelier in a way than the birds, which do need rather a lot of looking after. The four that arrived yesterday are still making a terrible row, and I'm afraid none of us got much sleep last night. Mummy says she wants to 'ring' their necks, which I didn't think very funny – though I know what she means. But I *love* the rings. Bless you for them. Love, Emily.

30 December:

Dear Edward – Whatever I expected to find when I opened the front door this morning, it certainly wasn't six socking great geese laying eggs all over the doorstep. Frankly, I rather hoped you had stopped sending me birds; we have no room for them and they have already ruined the croquet lawn. I know you meant well, but – let's call a halt, shall we? Love, Emily.

31 December:

Edward – I thought I said no more birds; this morning I find seven swans all trying to squeeze into our tiny goldfish pool. I'd rather not think what has happened to the goldfish. The whole house seems to be full of birds – to say nothing of what they leave behind them. Please, please, STOP. Your Emily.

1 January:

On balance, I prefer the birds. What on earth do you expect me to do with eight milkmaids – *and* their cows? Is this some kind of a joke? If so, I'm afraid I don't find it very amusing. Emily.

2 January:

Look here Edward, this has gone far enough. You say you're sending me nine ladies dancing; all I can say is that judging by the way they dance, they're certainly not ladies. This village just isn't accustomed to seeing a regiment of shameless hussies cavorting around the Green with nothing on but their lipstick – and it's Mummy and I who get the blame. If you value our friendship – which, I may say, I do less and less – kindly stop this ridiculous behaviour at once. Emily.

3 January:

As I write this letter, ten disgusting old men are prancing about all over what used to be the garden – before the geese and the swans and the cows got at it; and several of them, I notice, are taking inexcusable liberties with the milkmaids. Meanwhile the neighbours are trying to have us evicted. I shall never speak to you again. Emily.

4 January:

This is the last straw. You know I detest bagpipes. The place has now become something between a menagerie and a madhouse, and a man from the Council has just declared it unfit for habitation. At least Mummy has been spared this last outrage; they took her away yesterday afternoon in an ambulance. I hope you're satisfied. Emily.

5 January:

Sir - Our client, Miss Emily Wilbraham, instructs me to inform you that with the arrival on her premises at half past seven this morning of the entire percussion section of the Royal Liverpool Philharmonic Orchestra and several of their friends she has no course left open to her but to seek an injunction to prevent your importuning her further. I am making arrangements for the return of much assorted livestock.

I am, Sir,
Yours faithfully,
G Creep, Solicitor at Law.

A Christmas Cracker

2005

Two lovely pieces about translation. The first is by Miles Smith, in the Preface to the King James's Bible:

Translation it is that openeth the window, to let in the light; that breaketh the shell, that we may eat the kernel; that putteth aside the curtain, that we may look into the most Holy place: that removeth the cover of the well, that we may come by the water.

The second is from John Donne's 'Devotions':

All Mankind is of one Author, and is in one volume; when one Man dies, one Chapter is not torn out of the book, but translated into a better language; and every Chapter must be so translated; God employs several translators; some pieces are translated by age, some by sickness, some by war, some by justice; but God's hand is in every translation; and his hand shall bind up all our scattered leaves again, for that library where every book shall lie open to one another.

Some years ago the late and sorely missed Maggie Jencks (née Keswick) sent me a copy of the earliest – but for all I know still official – translation of the Japanese Highway Code, *as delivered to her grandmother in Yokohama when she became the first woman in Japan to hold a driving licence.*

Rules of the Road in Japan

At the rise of the hand of policeman, stop rapidly. Do not pass him by or otherwise disrespect him.

When a passenger of the foot hove in sight, tootle the horn trumpet to him melodiously at first. If he still obstacles your passage, tootle him with vigour and express by word of mouth the warning, 'Hi, Hi'.

Beware of the wandering horse that shall not pass and take fright as you pass him. Do not explode the (explode) exhaust box at him. Go soothingly by, or stop by the road-way till he pass away.

Give big space to the festive dog that makes sport in the roadway. Avoid entanglement of the dog with your wheelspokes.

Go soothingly on the grease-mud, as there lurk the skid demon. Press the brake of the foot as you roll around the corners to save the collapse and tie-up.

Sir John Gilbert, son of Sir Humphrey Gilbert the founder of Newfoundland, accompanied his uncle Sir Walter Ralegh to Guiana in 1595 and brought back a parrot, which he sent to Queen Elizabeth at her request. It was accompanied by the following letter, which was addressed to Sir Robert Cecil, Principal Secretary of State, and was dated 27 April 1596.

I have sent this bearer, my servant, of purpose unto you with the parakito, and have given him a great charge for the carrying of him. He will eat all kinds of meat and nothing will hurt him except it be very salt. If you put him on the table at meal time he will make choice of his meat. He must be kept very warm, and after he hath filled himself he will set in a gentlewoman's ruff all the day. In the afternoon he will eat bread or oatmeal groats, drink water or claret wine; every night he is put in the cage and covered warm. My servant more at large will tell you of all his conditions and qualities. Surely if he be well taught he will speak anything.

I can't quite resist comparing this letter with another, written – with, in its way, a similar purpose – to Pope Julius II:

The bearer of these gifts is Michelangelo the sculptor. His nature is such that he has to be drawn out by kindness and encouragement, but if he is treated well and if love be shown to him, he will accomplish things that will make the whole world wonder.

The Very Revd. Michael Mayne found the following footnote to 'On the Laws of Poetic Art', by Anthony Hecht, and was kind enough to send it on to me. It comes from an Irish newspaper of 1793.

THEATRE ROYAL, KILKENNY, IRELAND (Irish players). On Saturday, May 4, will be performed by command of several respectable people in the learned metropolis, for the benefit of Mr Kearns, the tragedy of HAMLET, originally written and composed by the celebrated DAN HAYES of LIMERICK, and inserted in Shakespeare's works. HAMLET by Mr Kearns (being his first appearance in that character) who, between the acts, will perform several solos on the potent bag-pipes, which play two tunes at the same time. OPHELIA by Mrs Prior, who will introduce several familiar airs in character, particularly THE LASS OF RICHMOND HILL and WE'LL ALL BE HAPPY TOGETHER from the Rev. Mr Dibdin's ODDITIES. The parts of the KING and QUEEN, by direction of the Rev. Mr O'Callagan, will be omitted, as too immoral for any stage. POLONIUS, the comical politician, by a Young Gentleman, being his first appearance in public. THE GHOST, THE GRAVEDIGGER and LAERTES, by Mr Sampson, the great London comedian. The characters will be dressed by Roman Shapes.

To which will be added an interlude of sleight of hand tricks, by the celebrated surveyor, Mr Hunt. The whole to conclude with a farce, MAHOMET THE IMPOSTER, Mahomet by Mr Kearns.

Tickets to be had of Mr Kearns at the sign of the Goat's Beard, in Castle Street. The value of the tickets to be taken (if required) in candles, butter, cheese, soap, etc., as Mr Kearns wishes in every particular to accommodate the public. No person will be admitted to the boxes without shoes or stockings.

The life that I have
Is all that I have
And the life that I have
Is yours

The love that I have
Of the life that I have
Is yours and yours and yours

The sleep I shall have
A rest I shall have
Yet death will be but a pause

For the peace of my years
In the long green grass
Will be yours and yours and yours.

This verse, sent to me by Dr Kenneth Sinclair-Loutit, was the individual code of the heroine of the French resistance Violette Szabo. It was written for her – one of many poems, apparently, that he wrote for his fellow-agents – by the chief code-maker for Special Operations Executive, Leo Marks.

    When I had a drink with Mr Marks on 19 February 1997, he told me that it had actually been written for an earlier love of his, Ruth Hambro, who had been killed in a plane crash in Canada. But he made no secret of the fact that he had been in love with Violette; when he gave her the poem and made her learn it by heart, he described it to her as 'a simple statement of fact'.

    He seemed reluctant to explain just how the poem was used, but brought with him what appeared to be a silk scarf which had been hers; on close inspection it proved to be covered with microscopic letters. He told me that he was writing a book, in which all would be made clear. (The book, 'Between Silk and Cyanide', has since been published and I have read it, but still don't altogether understand.)

When Violette Szabo was dropped into France on the night of 6-7 June 1944 she was almost immediately taken prisoner, though only after providing covering fire for her companion who got away. She survived in Nazi hands until well after the liberation of France, but was shot in Ravensbruck on 26 January 1945 by SS Schaarführer Schwartzhuber, who was later hanged. She was awarded a posthumous George Cross.

From the Diary of the Rev. Francis Kilvert, 22 April 1876:

As we came down the lower slopes of the wooded hillside into the glades of the park the herds of deer were moving under the brown oaks and the brilliant green hawthorns, and we came upon the tallest largest stateliest ash I ever saw and what seemed first in the dusk to be a great ruined grey tower; but which proved to be the vast ruin of the king oak of Moccas Park, hollow and broken but still alive and vigorous in parts and actually pushing out new shoots and branches. That tree may be 2000 years old. It measured roughly 33 feet round by arm stretching.

I fear those grey old men of Moccas, those grey, gnarled, low-browed, knock-kneed, bowed, bent, huge, strange, long-armed, deformed, hunch-backed, misshapen oak men that stand waiting and watching century and century, biding God's time with both feet in the grave and yet tiring down and seeing out generation after generation, with such tales to tell, as when they whisper them to each other in the mid-summer nights, make the silver birches weep and the poplars and aspens shiver and the long ears of the hares and rabbits stand on end. No human hand set those oaks. They are 'the tree which the Lord hath planted'. They look as if they had been at the beginning and making of the world, and they will probably see its end.

The longest palindrome? In Hubert Phillips's Heptameron *Mr Phillips gives us the following:*

> Puma, Puma! Iris won!
>   (Mural art)
> Puck-cap I was – lived a don
>   (No mural, mural art)
> Nor I, pater, if, as no slender stem, meek
>   I lose – beware dew!
> O vassal, can I wonder? Red is a star;
>   evil partner – wallahs deified.
> Shall a wren trap live rats? As I'd erred now
>   In a class-avowed era?
> We be so like emmets . . .
>   Red Nelson's afire – tap iron!
> *Tralarum, larum!* On nod, a devil saw I.
>   Pack cup!
> *Tralarum!* Now, sir, I am up –
>   Am up!

Some years ago my friend Ian Skidmore lent me a remarkable collection of pamphlets bound into a volume entitled Intemperance and Tight Lacing, Considered in Relation to the Laws of Life *by one O.S. Fowler, editor of the 'American Phrenological Journal'. It was published in London in 1849, and the title page carries the epigraph* Total Abstinence, or No Husbands – Natural Waists, or No Wives. *After seven closely-written pages on the evils of corseting, he writes:*

My conscience constrains me reluctantly to allude here to one another evil connected with tight-lacing . . . Who does not know that the compression of any part produces *inflammation!* Who does not know that, *therefore,* tight-lacing around the waist keeps the blood *from* returning freely to the heart, and *retains* it in the bowels and neighbouring organs, and thereby *inflames all the organs of the abdomen,* which thereby EXCITES AMATIVE DESIRES? Away goes this book into the fire! 'Shame! shame on the man who writes this!' exclaims Miss Fastidious Small-Waist. 'The man who wrote that, ought to be tarred and feathered!' Granted: and then what shall be done to the *woman* who *laces tight?* If it be improper for a man to *allude* to this *effect* of lacing, what is it for a *woman* to *cause* and *experience* it? Let me tell you, Miss Fastidious, that the less you say about this, the better; because I have TRUTH on my side, and because it is high time *that men who wish virtuous wives, knew it,* so that they may *avoid* those who have *inflamed* and exhausted this element of their nature.

To every man who prefers burying his children to the trouble or expense of raising them, I say, *marry a small waist,* and you will be sure to have few mature offspring, and those few thinned out by death.

No tongue can tell the number of mothers and children killed outright, or else made to drag out a short and miserable existence . . . Most effectually does it cramp, and girt in, and deaden the vital apparatus, and thus stop the flow of vitality at its fountain head . . . Yes, and that even by *Christian* mothers

– by the daughters of Zion, the followers of Jesus! Yea, more. These infanticides, *with their corsets actually on,* are admitted into the sanctuary of the Most High God, and even to the communion-table of the saints!

Another pamphlet in the same volume is entitled Amativeness; or, Evils and Remedies of Excessive and Perverted Sexuality. *In the section on* Matrimonial Excess *we read:*

But what stamps effectually the seal of nature's reprobation on excessive matrimonial indulgence, is its *destruction of the health of woman.* Is it not a most prolific cause of those distressing female complaints which *bury half our married women prematurely,* and seriously impair most of the remainder? . . . Speak out, ye weakly nervous wives, now dying by wretched inches of these diseases and say whether your sufferings were not caused mainly, and have not been aggravated to their present painfullness, by the frequency, the fury, the almost *goatishness,* of your husband's demands? Reader, if thou knowest none such, thou knowest not the *cause* of all the deaths that transpire around thee!

On the Vanity of Earthly Greatness

The tusks that clashed in mighty brawls
Of mastodons, are billiard balls.

The sword of Charlemagne the just
Is ferric oxide – known as rust.

The grizzly bear, whose potent hug
Was feared by all, is now a rug.

Great Caesar's dead, and on the shelf;
And I don't feel so well, myself.

                                    Arthur Guiterman

A letter from Sir John Betjeman to Miss Jane Boulenger, whom he believed – I suspect wrongly – to be French. It was found by John Guest in the archives of John Murray:

6/5/65

Chere M'lle,
J'ai correcté les typescripts. A la meme temps j'ai made a list of suitable illustrations que je suis keeping pour aide memoire quand nous come to review le whole libre.

Cest tres important pour emphasise au le Major que les illustrations sont tres importants, aussi make-up. J'implore lui ne settez anything up in type until we discuss format et whether je suis going to be allowed couleur aussi whether le libre est not trop plein de discontent & sur la meme note. Aussi comme far ce serai possible departer from photographs.

Au revoir
Sean O'betjeman

Sunday Morning

There's one joins sweetly in the quavering hymn,
Hears prayer and reading, never lets a sigh,
Christian in docile breath and breast and limb,
But pagan in the corner of her eye.

L.A.G. Strong

A rather different prime ministerial obituary, from pen alas unknown, has been supplied by my friend Nicolas Barker:

> Lloyd George no doubt
> When his life ebbs out
> Will be off to Hell in a chariot,
> Sitting in state
> On a red-hot plate
> Twixt Satan and Judas Iscariot.
> Ananias that day
> To Beelzebub will say
> 'My claim to precedence fails!
> So move me up higher
> Away from the fire
> And make room for that liar from Wales.

(In the original Cracker I had 'And the Devil' in line 7 instead of 'Ananias', and 'that bugger from Wales' instead of 'that liar from Wales.'

Nicolas subsequently wrote, in a mock-pompous letter:

'You will recall that Welshmen are all liars and that L.G. was the quintessential Welshman, as Ananias was (see the Acts of the Apostles) the first person in Holy Writ to receive condign punishment for LYING. But even one tone-deaf could not miss the necessity of rhyming 'higher' and 'fire' with a third assonance. 'Bugger' is an outrage to poetry far exceeding that to good taste. Furthermore you will surely agree that L.G. was far too busily engaged otherwise to find time for sodomy.'

As a penultimate postscript, I might add that I received a message from – of all places – Papua-New Guinea, to the effect that these lines are a plagiarism of an older obituary coined by a wit of Corpus Christi College, Oxford, for its quondam Master Edward Perowne, 'a Victorian Divine of severe mien and, one suspects, possibly an equally severe humour':

Teddy Perowne
Is gone to his own,
Is gone to his own in a chariot;
And he sits there in state
On a fizzing-hot plate
Between Pontius and Judas Iscariot.')

*Finally, I should quote from a letter recently received from my friend
Philip Brunette:*

On one occasion Lloyd George addressed a meeting in a small
Welsh village where he was introduced by one of the deacons of the
local chapel as follows:

'We all know the remarks made on this subject last week by
the Bishop of St. Asaph, who in my opinion is the biggest liar
in creation. Fortunately we have here tonight Mr. David Lloyd
George, who will be more than a match for him.'

And while we are on the subject of Hell, here is a piece kindly sent me by Isabella Gardiner. It seems that a chemistry mid-term examination paper set by the University of Washington contained a bonus question: 'Is Hell exothermic (gives off heat) or endothermic (absorbs heat)?' A student submitted the following answer:

First, we need to know how the mass of Hell is changing in time. So we need to know that rate at which souls are moving into Hell and the rate at which they are leaving.

I think that we can safely assume that once a soul gets to Hell it will not leave. Therefore, no souls are leaving.

As for how many souls are entering Hell, let's look at the different religions that exist in the world today. Some of these religions state that if you are not a member of their religion you will go to Hell. Since there are more than one of these religions and since people do not belong to more than one religion, we can project that all souls go to Hell. With birth and death rates as they are, we can expect the number of souls in Hell to increase exponentially.

Now we look at the rate of change of the volume of Hell, because Boyle's law states that in order for the temperature and pressure to stay the same, the volume has to expand proportionately as souls are added.

This gives two possibilities:

1. If Hell is expanding at a slower rate than the rate at which souls enter Hell, then the temperature and pressure in Hell will increase until all Hell breaks loose.
2. If Hell is expanding at a rate faster than the increase of souls in Hell, then the temperature and pressure will drop until Hell freezes over.

So which is it?

If we accept the postulate given me by Teresa during my freshman year, '. . . that it will be a cold day in Hell before I sleep with you', and take into account the fact that I still have not succeeded in having sexual relations with her, then No. 2 cannot be true; and thus I am sure that Hell is endothermic and will not freeze.

The author received, we are told, the only 'A' given.

(Michael Pakenham has submitted an alternative, which I prefer:

'If we accept the postulate given to me by Teresa during my freshman year, that 'it will be a cold day in Hell before I sleep with you', and take account of the fact that I slept with her last night, then the second possibility must be true. This proves that Hell is exothermic and has already frozen over.

The corollary of this theory is that since Hell has frozen over, it follows that it is no longer accepting any more souls and is therefore extinct. This leaves only Heaven, thereby proving the existence of a Divine Being. Which in turn explains why last night Teresa kept shouting 'Oh my God!')

From Hell to Paradise. Milton's account, in Book IX of Paradise Lost, *of Satan's approach to Eve makes me understand for the first time why she fell such an easy victim:*

> So spake the Enemie of Mankind, enclos'd
> In Serpent, Inmate bad, and toward Eve
> Addressed his way, not with indented wave,
> Prone on the ground, as since, but on his reare,
> Circular base of rising foulds, that tour'd [*towered*]
> Fould above fould a surging Maze, his Head
> Crested aloft, and Carbuncle his Eyes;
> With burnish't Neck of verdant Gold, erect
> Amidst his circling Spires, that on the grass
> Floted redundant: pleasing was his shape,
> And lovely, never since Serpent Kind
> Lovelier . . . .
> . . . . .with tract oblique
> At first, as one who sought access, but feared
> To interrupt, side-long he works his way.
> As when a Ship by skilful Stearsman wrought
> Nigh River's mouth or Foreland, where the Wind
> Veres oft, as oft so steers, and shifts her Saile;
> So varied Hee, and of his tortuous Traine
> Curl'd many a wanton wreath in sight of Eve,
> To lure her Eye; shee busied heard the sound
> Of rushing Leaves, but minded not, as us'd
> To such disport before her through the Field,
> From every Beast, more duteous at her call,
> Than at Circean call the Herd disguis'd.
> Hee boulder now, uncall'd before her stood;
> But as in gaze admiring: Oft he bow'd
> His turret Crest, and sleek enamel'd Neck,
> Fawning, and lick'd the ground whereon she trod.
> His gentle dumb expression turn'd at length
> The Eye of Eve to mark his play; he glad
> Of her attention gain'd, with Serpent Tongue

Organic, or impulse of vocal Air,
His fraudulent temptation then began.

But even Milton sometimes nods. In the 1987 Cracker I quoted
Adam's unfortunate reference, when in conversation with Eve, to

Our walks at noon, with branches overgrown,
That mock our scant manuring.

And there is also a memorable image to be found in Samson Agonistes:

Then with what trivial weapon came to hand,
The Jaw of a dead Ass, his sword of bone,
A thousand fore-skins fell, the flower of *Palestin*
In *Ramath-lechi* famous to this day.

A letter from Dickens to his clockmaker:

My dear Sir,

Since my hall clock was sent to your establishment to be cleaned it has gone (as indeed it always has) perfectly well, but has struck the hours with great reluctance, and after enduring internal agonies of a most distressing nature, it has now ceased striking altogether. Though a happy release for the clock, this is not convenient to the household. If you can send down any confidential person with whom the clock can confer, I think it may have something on its works it would be glad to make a clean breast of.

Faithfully yours
Charles Dickens

*In the Cracker for 1994, under the heading ALTERNATIVE
ENDINGS TO AN UNWRITTEN BALLAD, I quoted a number
of quatrains describing various sightings of the sinister Mrs Ravoon.
Over the last decade, I am glad to announce that there have been
several more. The ever-vigilant Linda Kelly has notched up two:*

> I was leaving a party near Regent's Canal,
> Where I merrily chatted to many a pal.
> When I looked for my jacket I fell in a swoon –
> Impaled on the coat hook was . . . MRS RAVOON.

and

> The General's inspection had gone very well
> Till the barracks commander cried out 'What the hell . . . ?
> Recumbent upstairs 'neath a cashiered dragoon,
> Half blotto and snoring, lay . . . MRS RAVOON.

Geoffrey Wilde reported:

> His victims had numbered some fifty or more,
> But now one single shot saw him fall to the floor;
> So who would emerge from that western saloon?
> Gun smoking, unsmiling, strode . . . MRS RAVOON.

But the ultimate sighting came from Robin Wilson:

> At the end of the universe, lost in the void,
> The continuum's crumbling and time is destroyed:
> Then, clear through the chaos, a solo bassoon:
> Is it Gabriel's horn? No, it's . . . MRS RAVOON.

From Winston Churchill's tribute to Neville Chamberlain. House of Commons, 12 November 1940:

The fierce and bitter controversies which hung around him in recent times were hushed by the news of his illness and silenced by his death. In paying a tribute of respect and of regard to an eminent man who has been taken from us, no one is obliged to alter the opinions which he has formed or expressed upon issues which have become a part of history; but at the Lychgate we may all pass our own conduct and our own judgements under a searching review. It is not given to human beings, happily for them, for otherwise life would be intolerable, to foresee or to predict to any large extent the unfolding course of events. In one phase men seem to have been right, in another they seem to have been wrong. Then again, a few years later, when the perspective of time has lengthened, all stands in a different setting. There is a new proportion. There is another scale of values. History with its flickering lamp stumbles along the trail of the past, trying to reconstruct its scenes, to revive its echoes, and kindle with pale gleams the passion of former days. What is the worth of all this? The only guide to a man is his conscience; the only shield to his memory is the rectitude and sincerity of his actions. It is very imprudent to walk through life without this shield, because we are so often mocked by the failure of our hopes and the upsetting of our calculations; but with this shield, however the fates may play, we march always in the ranks of honour.

Another more than welcome contribution from Isabella. On this two hundredth anniversary of the Battle of Trafalgar, the following dialogue may seem a melancholy reflection on our own times:

Nelson: Order the signal, Hardy.

Hardy: Aye, Aye, Sir.

N: Hold on, that's not what I told the Signal Officer. What's the meaning of this Hardy? 'England expects every person to do their duty, regardless of race, gender, sexual orientation, religious persuasion or disability' What gobbledygook is this?

H: Admiralty policy, I'm afraid sir. We're an equal opportunities employer now. We had a devil of a job getting 'England' past the censors, lest it be considered racist.

N: Gazooks, Hardy. Hand me my pipe and tobacco.

H: Sorry, sir. All naval vessels have been designated smoke free working environments.

N: In that case break open the rum ration. Let us splice the mainbrace to steel the men before battle.

H: The rum ration has been abolished, Admiral. The government is against binge drinking.

N: Good heavens Hardy. Well get on with it. Full speed ahead.

H: I think you will find there is a 4 knot speed limit in this stretch of water, sir.

N: Dammit man, we are on the eve of the greatest sea battle in history. We must advance with all despatch. Report from the crow's nest Hardy.

H: That won't be possible, sir.

N: What?

H: Health and Safety have closed the crow's nest, sir. No harness, and the rope ladder doesn't meet regulations. They won't let anyone up there until proper scaffolding has been erected.

N: Then get me the ship's carpenter without delay, Hardy.

H: He's busy knocking up a wheelchair access to the fo'c'sle, Admiral.

N: Wheelchair access? This is absurd.

H: Health and Safety again, sir. We have to provide a barrier free environment for the differently abled.

N: Differently abled? I've only one arm and one eye – I didn't rise to the rank of Admiral by playing the disability card.

H: Actually you did, sir. The Royal Navy is under represented in the area of visual impairment and limb deficiency.

N: Whatever next? Give full sail, Hardy. The salt spray beckons.

H: Couple of problems there too, sir. Health and Safety won't let the crew up the rigging without crash helmets: and they don't want anyone breathing in too much salt.

N: I've never heard such infamy. Break out the cannon and tell the men to stand by to engage the enemy.

H: The men are a bit worried about shooting at anyone, Admiral.

N: What's this, Hardy? Mutiny?

H: It's not that, sir, but they are afraid of being charged with felony. There's a couple of legal aid lawyers on board watching everyone like hawks.

N: Then how are we supposed to sink the Frenchies and the Spanish?

H: Actually, sir, we're not.

N: We're not?

H: No, sir. The Frenchies and the Spanish are our European partners now: and according to the Common Fisheries Policy, we shouldn't even be in this stretch of water. We could get hit for compensation.

N: But we hate the French and anybody who speaks ill of the King.

H: I wouldn't let the ship's diversity co-ordinator hear you saying that, sir. We must be inclusive in this multicultural age. You'll be up on a disciplinary. Now, put on your Kevlar vest, it's the rules.

N: Don't tell me, health and safety. What ever happened to Rum, the Lash and Sodomy?

H: As I explained, sir – rum is off and there is a ban on corporal punishment.

N: Kiss me Hardy.

A jolly little story told of Dr Thomas Arne (1710-78), composer of 'Rule Britannia':

He further managed to acquire some proficiency on the violin, and soon contrived to get some lessons from the accomplished and eminent violinist, Michael Festing . . . Calling in King Street one day for this purpose, Festing found Arne diligently practising with his music supported on the lid of a coffin. Horrified at the sight, he declared he could not play under such circumstances, as he would be constantly imagining there might be a corpse in the coffin beneath. 'So there is,' said Arne, and gave proof by removing the lid.

In 1970 – it was my first-ever Cracker – I quoted some really bad poetry, including what I suggested were perhaps the most atrocious opening lines ever written. Both are by Wordsworth, and both owe their atrociousness to the inclusion of modern surnames. The first is from a sonnet rather endearingly entitled 'To the Spade of a Friend'.

Spade! With which Wilkinson hath tilled his lands . . .

The other, addressed to one of the leading abolitionists of the slave trade, runs it close:

Clarkson! It was an obstinate hill to climb:

(Its continuation strikes me as very little better:

How toilsome – nay, how dire it was, by thee
Is known; by none perhaps so feelingly.)

Since then I have come across several more examples. How about Chatterton's

The blood-stained tomb where Smith and comfort lie

or Crabbe's

And I was asked and authorised to go
To seek the firm of Clutterbuck and Co.

Finally, by Isaac Watts:
Heaven was impatient of our crimes,
    And sent his minister of death
To scourge the bold rebellion of the times,
    And to demand our Prophet's breath;
He came commissioned for the fates
Of awful Mead and charming Bates;
There he essayed the vengeance first,
Then took dismal aim, and brought great Gouge to dust.

Anya Sainsbury has kindly sent me this extract from the 'Deaths' column of The Times *of 28 February 2003:*

On this day in 1844 President John Tyler, Cabinet officials and other dignitaries boarded the American warship *Princeton* for a cruise on the Potomac river to demonstrate one of the vessel's large guns, the Peacemaker. However, the cannon misfired and violently exploded, killing not only the Secretary of State, Abel Upshur, but also the Secretary of War, Thomas Gibson, and Senator David Gardiner. Julia Gardiner, the Senator's daughter, was thrown against President Tyler in the blast. Four months later she became First Lady.

My dear first wife Anne has sent me this extract from an article on Giacometti by Martin Gayford in the Sunday Telegraph *of 26 May 1996:*

The next year, 1939, [Giacometti] began working not from the model but from memory, and a bizarre thing happened. As he wrote to the dealer Pierre Matisse, 'to my terror the sculptures became smaller and smaller. These dimensions revolted me, and kept on beginning, only to end up a few months later at the same point' . . .

He continued to make his sculptures, which, do what he might, almost invariably dwindled away to almost nothing, when he would usually destroy them. At the end of 1941 he departed for his native Switzerland, promising not to return until his sculpture was less absurd in size. But it refused to grow. For the next three years he worked in a cheap hotel, caked in plaster dust, whittling away at sculptures scarcely larger than a pin, which almost never satisfied him.

He returned in September 1945 with three years' work in six matchboxes.

I sing of Brooks, of Blossomes, Birds and Bowers:
Of April, May, of June, and July-Flowers,
I sing of May-poles, Hock-carts, Wassails, Wakes;
Of Bride-grooms, Brides and of their Bridall-cakes.
I write of Youth, of Love, and have Accesse
By these, to sing of cleanly-wantonnesse.
I sing of Dewes, of Raines, and piece by piece,
Of Balme, of Oyle, of Spice, and Amber-gris.
I sing of Times trans-shifting, and I write
How roses first came Red, and Lillies White.
I write of Groves, of Twilights, and I sing
The Court of Mab, and of the Fairie-King.
I write of Hell; I sin (and ever shall)
Of Heaven, and hope to have it after all.

Robert Herrick
(1591-1674)

Swinburne said that Herrick was 'the greatest song-writer – as surely as Shakespeare is the greatest dramatist – ever born of English race'.

Southey, on the other hand, wrote that 'of all our poets this man appears to have had the coarsest mind. Without being intentionally obscene, he is thoroughly filthy, and has not the slightest sense of decency. In an old writer, and especially one of that age, I never saw so large a proportion of what may truly be called either trash or ordure.'

Be comforted, little dog; thou too at the resurrection shalt have a little golden tail.

Martin Luther

BONUS

From Bishop G.K.A. Bell's biography of Randall Davidson,
Archbishop of Canterbury 1903-28, Chapter IV:

In the centre of the Chapel [St George's Chapel, Windsor], midway between the Sovereign's stall and the high altar, lies a vault under a pavement made of squares of black and white marble. Within the vault are four royal coffins. The large leaden coffin of Henry VIII lies in the centre. On its south side, with a space of about three inches between their shoulders, lies the coffin of Charles I, covered still with a black velvet pall, which seems to be in good preservation. Upon the coffin of King Charles, near the foot, lies a little coffin covered with black cloth, containing the remains of an infant child of Queen Anne. At the north side of Henry VIII lies the small leaden coffin of Queen Jane Seymour.

In 1813, in the reign of King George III, the coffin of Charles I had, apparently with the connivance of the Dean of the day (Legge), been opened for inspection by the Prince Regent, Sir Henry Halford[1], his physician, and others. It would seem that certain articles were removed at the time, namely 1) a portion of the cervical vertebra cut transversely with some sharp instrument, 2) a portion of the beard of the King of auburn colour, with a bit of linen cerecloth attaching to it, 3) a tooth. In 1888, these relics were in the possession of Sir Henry Halford's grandson, Sir Henry St John Halford. He desired to restore them, and presented them in a small ebony box to the Prince of Wales. The box contained the following inscription, engraved on a plate inside the lid:

[1] See page 69.

En
Caroli I Regis
Ipsissimum os cervicis
Ferro eheu! intercisum
1648
Et regiam insuper barbam

Dean Davidson, with a view to their safety in the future, suggested to the Prince of Wales that he might think it right to replace these relics in the vault or grave from which they had been abstracted. The Prince of Wales agreed. The Queen was consulted, and her consent obtained, on condition that no one entered the vault or disturbed the coffin. The Prince handed the ebony box to the Dean on Tuesday, December 11; and the Dean had a leaden casket prepared, which was enclosed in a stout oaken case, fitting closely, and all firmly closed with screws, with the following inscription on the lid of the leaden casket:

The relics enclosed in this case were taken from the coffin of King Charles I on April 1, 1813, by Sir Henry Halford, Physician to King George III. They were by his grandson Sir Henry Halford given to HRH Albert Edward, Prince of Wales.

On December 13th, 1888, they were replaced by HRH in this vault, their original resting-place.

The day appointed for the restoration was Thursday, December 13. After the service of Evensong, the Dean, with Canon Eliot as Canon in Residence, and Canon Dalton, superintended the removal of the pavement stones above the vault. This was done with the utmost care and reverence by Mr A.Y. Nutt, Surveyor to the Dean and Canons, and three workmen, and occupied a very short time. Six of the small squares of black and white marble were raised, with the mortar that lay between them, and the brick arch of the vault was removed. From this about twenty bricks were taken out with the greatest care so that no débris should fall on the coffin beneath. By this means an aperture of about eighteen inches square was made immediately over the centre of King Charles's coffin. The workmen retired from the Chapel as soon as the aperture had been made.

The Prince of Wales then came to the Chapel. It was just past seven o'clock and the choir was wrapped in darkness on the winter evening. Only a long coil of magnesium wire served to light the narrow chamber, in which the martyr King and his royal companions lay. All was silent as the little company of watchers gazed within; but no foot was allowed to enter. The Prince of Wales stooped down and lowered the ebony casket in its oaken case, with the relics, and placed it near the centre of King Charles's coffin. The Prince then withdrew. The workmen re-entered the Chapel, and thee aperture into the vault was closed. The opening in the brick arch was rebuilt from above, each brick being held in place by hand till the mortar had set. The marble pavement was relaid, and by half-past nine that night all had departed from the Chapel.

The part Dr Bell leaves out is fortunately provided by another, later, Dean of Windsor, A.V. Baillie. Writing in 1947 to Bishop A.A. David of Liverpool, in a letter preserved in the Lambeth Palace Library, he reports that

When they got there, no provision had been made for letting the box down. By tying all their handkerchiefs together a long enough cord was provided to enable the Prince, by lying flat on his stomach and reaching down, to land the box on the coffin. Davidson always said that it was the most amusing scene he ever witnessed. The next morning the vault was closed, and no whisper of what had happened got abroad.

A Christmas Cracker

 2006

I do not think I shall ever forget the sight of Etna at sunset: the mountain almost invisible in a blur of pastel grey, glowing on the top and then repeating its shape, as though reflected, in a wisp of grey smoke, with the whole horizon behind it radiant with pink light, fading gently into a grey pastel sky. Nothing I have ever seen in Art or Nature was quite so revolting.

Evelyn Waugh
Labels, 1929

From a letter to Francesco Vettori in Rome, from Niccolò Machiavelli:

I will tell you what my life is now. I get up in the morning with
the sun, and go into a wood of mine that I am having cut down.
I spend an hour or two there looking over the work done on the
previous day and passing the time with the woodcutters, who
always have some quarrel on their hands, among themselves or
with their neighbours . . .

When I leave the wood I go to a spring and on from there with
a book under my arm, Dante or Petrarch, or one of the minor
poets, Tibullus, Ovid or someone like that, to an *uccellare* which I
have. I read of their amorous passions and their loves; I remember
my own – and for a while these reflections make me happy. Then
I move on along the road to the inn, talking to passers-by, asking
news of the place they come from, hearing about this and that and
observing the various tastes and fancies of mankind. This brings me
to lunchtime, when I and my brood eat such food as this poor farm
and my slender patrimony provides. When I have eaten I go back
to the inn, where I usually find the landlord, a butcher, a miller and
couple of bakers. With these I act the rustic for the rest of the day,
playing at *cricca* and *tric-trac,* which lead to a thousand squabbles
and countless slanging-matches – our fights usually over a farthing,
but we can be heard shouting none the less from San Casciano . . .

When evening comes, I return home and go into my study. On
the threshold I strip off my muddy, sweaty, workday clothes and
put on the robes of court and palace, and in this graver dress I enter
the antique courts of the ancients and am welcomed by them, and
then I taste the food that alone is mine, and for which I was born.
And there I make bold to speak to them and ask the motives of
their actions; and they, in their humanity, reply to me. And for the
space of four hours I forget the world, remember no vexation, fear
poverty no more, tremble no more at death: I pass indeed into their
world.

We do not accept the producers' argument that 'Pink Pussy' and 'Screaming Orgasm' as names of drinks do not suggest any association with sexual success, still less that 'Shag' was simply a reference to a seabird.

Annual Report of the Portland Group

The eighty-four-year-old John Paul was laid out in the Clementine Hall, dressed in white and red vestments, his head covered with a white bishop's miter and propped up on three dark gold pillows.

Tucked under his left arm was the silver staff, called the crow's ear, that he had carried in public . . .

International Herald Tribune
4 April 2005

The world's first public steam railway, the Stockton-Darlington, opened in 1825; the second was the Liverpool-Manchester. This was launched on 25 August 1830; the engine pulling the invited guests was George Stephenson's Rocket, *capable of 31 m.p.h. Among them was the actress Fanny Kemble, who wrote an account of the trip:*

We were introduced to the little engine which was to drag us along the rails. She (for they make these curious little fire-horses all mares) consisted of a boiler, a stove, a small platform, a bench, and behind the bench a barrel containing enough water to prevent her being thirsty for fifteen miles – the whole machine not bigger than the common fire-engine. She goes upon two wheels, which are her feet, and are moved by bright steel legs called pistons; these are propelled by steam, and in proportion as more steam is applied to the upper extremities (the hip-joints, I suppose) of these pistons, the faster they move the wheels; and when it is desirable to diminish the speed, the steam, which unless suffered to escape would burst the boiler, evaporates through a safety-valve into the air. The reins, bit and bridle of this wonderful beast is a small steel handle, which applies or withdraws the steam from its legs or pistons, so that a child might manage it. The coals, which are its oats, were under the bench, and there was a small glass tube affixed to the boiler, with water in it, which indicates by its fullness or emptiness when the creature wants water, which is immediately conveyed to it from its reservoirs. There is a chimney to the stove, but as they burn coke there is none of that dreadful black smoke which accompanies the progress of a steam-vessel. The snorting little animal, which I felt inclined to pat, was then harnessed to our carriage, and Mr Stephenson having taken me on the bench of the engine with him, we started at about ten miles an hour . . .

The engine having received its supply of water, the carriage was placed behind it, for it cannot turn, and was set off at its utmost speed, thirty-five miles an hour, swifter than a bird flies (for they have tried the experiment with a snipe). You cannot conceive what the sensation of cutting the air was; the motion is as smooth as possible too. I could either have read or written; and as it was, I stood up, and with my bonnet off 'drank the air before me'. The wind, which was strong, or perhaps the force of our thrusting against it, absolutely weighed my eyelids down. When I closed my eyes this sensation of flying was quite delightful, and strange beyond description; yet, strange as it was, I had a perfect sense of security, and not the slightest fear.

A letter addressed to the Earl of Pembroke at the Foreign Office by Sir Archibald Clerk Kerr (later Lord Inverchapel), H.M. Ambassador in Moscow, on 6 April 1943:

My dear Reggie,

In these dark days a man tends to look for little shafts of light that spill from heaven. My days are probably darker than yours, and I need, my God I do, all the light I can get. But I am a decent fellow, and I do not want to be mean and selfish about what little brightness is shed upon me from time to time. So I propose to share with you a tiny flash that has illuminated my sombre life and tell you that god has given me a new Turkish colleague whose card tells me that he is called Mustafa Kunt.

We all feel like that, Reggie, now and then, especially when Spring is upon us, but few of us would care to put it on our cards. It takes a Turk to do that.

Archie

Notices for tourists abroad are often of singular interest. Here are a few:

Leipzig lift: Do not enter the lift backwards, and only when lit up.

Belgrade lift: To move the cabin, push button for wishing floor. If the cabin should enter more persons, each one should press a number of wishing floor. Driving is then going alphabetically by national order.

Serbian hotel: The flattening of underwear with pleasure is the job of the chambermaid.

Japanese hotel: You are invited to take advantage of the chambermaid.

Austrian ski hotel: Not to perambulate the corridors in the hours of repose in the boots of ascension.

Swiss *menu:* Our wines leave you nothing to hope for.

Zurich hotel: Because of the impropriety of entertaining guests of the opposite sex in the bedroom, it is suggested that the lobby be used for this purpose.

Polish menu: Salad a firm's own make; limpid red beet soup with cheesy dumplings in the form of a finger; roasted duck let loose; beef rashers beaten up in the country people's fashion.

Black Forest Camp Site: It is strictly forbidden that people of different sex, for instance men and women, live together in one tent unless they are married with each other for that purpose.

Rome laundry: Ladies, leave your clothes here and spend the afternoon having a good time.

Czech tourist agency: Take one of our horse-driven city tours – we guarantee no miscarriages.

Donkey rides in Thailand: Would you like to ride on your own ass?

Traffic sign in Kyushi, Japan: Stop: drive sideways.

Swiss mountain inn: Special today: no ice cream.

Bangkok temple: It is forbidden to enter a woman even a foreigner if dressed as a man.

Tokyo bar: Special cocktails for ladies with nuts.

Moscow hotel room: If this is your first visit to the USSR, you are welcome to it.

Norwegian cocktail bar: Ladies are required not to have children in the bar.

Acapulco hotel: The Manager has personally passed all the water served here.

Something called *M25: The Movie* shows a clockwise drive round the 128 miles of motorway on a Sunday. There is no commentary, only the hum of the engine. The highlight is a glimpse of a man mending a lamp. Nevertheless, 300 copies of the £9.99 video went in just two weeks by mail order in February 1993. A sequel, *M25: The Film*, showing the orbital wonder in the other direction, had a sparse spoken soundtrack and clearly lacked the austere formalism of the original. It was a mail-order disaster.

The Sunday Telegraph
16 April 2000

CRAFTSMEN

All craftsmen share a knowledge. They have held
Reality down fluttering to a bench;
Cut wood to their own purposes; compelled
The growth of pattern with the patient shuttle;
Drained acres to a trench.
Control is theirs. They have ignored the subtle
Release of spirit from the jail shape.
They have been concerned with prison, not escape;
Pinioned the fact, and let the rest go free,
And out of need made inadvertent art.
All things designed to play a faithful part
Build up their plain particular poetry.
Tools have their own integrity:
The sheath of scythe curves rightly in the hand,
The hammer knows its balance; knife its edge,
All tools inevitably planned,
Stout friends, with pledge
Of service; with their crochets too
That masters understand,
And proper character, and separate heart,
But always to their chosen temper true.
– So language, smithied at the common fire,
Grew to its use; as sneath and shank and haft
Of well-grained wood, nice instruments of craft,
Curve to the simple mould the hands require,
Born of the needs of man.
The poet like the artisan
Works lonely with his tools; picks up each one,
Blunt mallet knowing, and the quick thin blade,
And plane that travels when the hewing's done;
Rejects, and chooses; scores a fresh faint line:

Sharpens, intent upon his chiselling:
Bends lower to examine his design,
If it be truly made,
And brings perfection to so slight a thing.
But in the shadows of his working place,
Dust-moted, dim,
Among the chips and lumber of his trade,
Lifts never his bowed head, a breathing-space
To look upon the world beyond the sill,
The world framed small, in distance, for to him
The world and all its weight are in his will.
Yet in the ecstasy of his rapt mood
There's no retreat his spirit cannot fill,
No distant leagues, no present, and no past,
No essence that his need may not distil,
All pressed into his service, but he knows
Only the immediate care, if that be good;
The little focus that his words enclose;
As the poor joiner, working at his wood,
Knew not the tree from which the planks were taken,
Knew not the glade from which the trunk was brought,
Knew not the soil in which the roots were fast,
Nor by what centuries of gales the boughs were shaken,
But holds them all beneath his hands at last.

Victoria Sackville-West

On the Sultan Ibrahim, who succeeded to the Ottoman throne in 1640:

As Murat [his predecessor] was wholly addicted to wine, so was Ibrahim to lust. They say he spent all his time in sensual pleasure and when nature was exhausted with the frequent repetition of venereal delights he endeavored to restore it with potions or commanded a beautiful virgin richly habited to be brought to him by his mother, the Grand Vezir, or some other great man. He covered the walls of his chamber with looking-glass so that his love battles might seem to be enacted at several places at once. He ordered his pillows to be stuffed with rich furs, so that the bed designed for the imperial pleasure might be the more precious. Nay, he put whole sable skins under him in a notion that his lust would be inflamed if his love toil were rendered more difficult by the glowing of his knees. In the palace gardens, he frequently assembled all the virgins, made them strip themselves naked, and neighing like a stallion ran among them and . . . ravished one or the other, kicking or struggling by his order. Happening once to see the privy parts of a wild heifer he sent the shape of them in gold all over the Empire with orders to make enquiry whether a woman made just in that manner could be found for his lust. At last such a one was found and received into the women's apartments. He made a collection of great and voluminous books of pictures expressing the various ways of coition whence he ever invented some new and previously unknown postures. Thus the public treasury, earlier diminished by Murat's drunkenness, was quite exhausted by Ibrahim's luxury and lust, and the sinews of the Empire which were applied by his ancestors to repulse their enemies and enlarge their domains, were by him used to the destruction of his body.

Demetrius Cantemir
*History of the Growth and Decay
of the Ottoman Empire*, London, 1756

Two of my favourite gems from P.G. Wodehouse:

Nothing so surely introduces a sour note into a wedding ceremony as the abrupt disappearance of the groom in a cloud of dust.

A Pelican at Blandings

You'd remember all right if you'd had a mint julep in America. Insidious things. They creep up on you like a baby sister and slide their little hands into yours and the next thing you know the judge is telling you to pay the clerk of the court fifty dollars.

Summer Lightning

A whole collection could be made of descriptions of the effects of alcohol on the unwary. Irvin S. Cobb wrote of corn liquor:

A sudden violent jolt of it has been known to stop the victim's watch, snap his suspenders and crack his glass eye right across.

The Revd. David Burton Evans sends me this extract from the minutes of the Annual General Meeting of the Elgar Society, July 2005:

Chairman Andrew Neill welcomed members to the meeting, in particular those attending for the first time and members from overseas. He regretted that the Society had no members in South America, where he felt that musical life was clearly exciting. He had read the following story from a recent issue of *Music Business Magazine:*

'Paulo Esperanza, bass trombonist with the Uruguayan Symphony Orchestra, decided to make his own contribution to the cannon shots fired as part of the Orchestra's performance of Tchaikovsky's *1812 Overture.* He placed a large ignited firecracker, equivalent to a quarter stick of dynamite, into an aluminium straight mute and then inserted the mute into the bell of his trombone.

'Later, from his hospital bed, Mr Esperanza explained: 'I thought the bell of my trombone would shield me from the explosion and focus the blast outwards.' In his haste to get his trombone up before the firecracker went off, he failed to elevate the bell high enough to give the mute sufficient arc to clear the orchestra. As a result the mute streaked through the woodwind and viola sections before slamming into the stomach of the conductor and knocking him off the podium into the audience. The folding chairs of the front row collapsed, setting off a domino effect, toppling row after row of chairs.

'Back on stage, the blast of the firecracker sent a surge of super-heated gas through the trombone to propel the slide, like a spear, into the head of an unsuspecting third clarinettist, knocking him unconscious and fracturing his skull.'

The more formal part of the A.G.M. then got under way.

There are in England nymphs of divine appearance, both
engaging and agreeable, whom you would certainly prefer to
your Muses; and there is, besides, one custom which can never
be commended too highly. When you arrive anywhere, you are
received with kisses on all sides, and when you take your leave they
speed you on your way with kisses. The kisses are renewed when
you come back. When guests come to your house, their arrival is
pledged with kisses; and when they leave, kisses are shared once
again. If you should happen to meet, then kisses are given profusely.
In a word, wherever you turn, the world is full of kisses.

Erasmus of Rotterdam
(from his first letter from England, 1499)

From an illustrated booklet in the possession of my daughter Artemis and entitled THE PYONGYANG METRO, published by Korea Pictorial, Pyongyang, D.P.R.K.:

One day in September 1968, respected President Kim Il Sung visited a pitface of the construction of the metro and gave guidance to the project for many hours. He looked at the stairs to the entrance of the pit and stepped on the steep stairs one by one to the end.

In this way the happiness of the people was provided by the goodness of the President, who took the trouble of the people into his first consideration . . .

On September 5, 1973, there took place an opening ceremony of the Pyongyang Metro. That day the great leader President Kim Il Sung said to officials in a thoughtful tone before cutting the red tape hanging down in the place for opening ceremony.

'I think it is difficult to build the metro, but it is not to cut the tape.'

Hearing his words, who considered the trouble of builders first, the participants in the opening ceremony felt a lump in their throats and gave enthusiastic cheers, waving the bundles of flowers.

Simon Raison has been good enough to send me the following extract from the catalogue, dated July 2002, of Messrs Tindley & Chapman, booksellers:

211. MORGAN, EVAN A. *A Sequence of Seven Sonnets.* Brown wrappers. Very nice. Elkin Matthews, 1920. The author was an exotic figure even for the times. Among his foibles were a penchant for dressing up in the guise of the travel writer Rosita Forbes, teaching his pet kangaroo to box and owning a parakeet that he liked to keep down his trousers. The short foreword by Wilfred Childe contains more pretentious drivel in three paragraphs than most people could pen in a lifetime.

On Friday May 26 2006 a statue of King Ethelbert of Kent (556-616) was unveiled at Canterbury and placed next to a similar statue, erected in 2005, of his French wife Queen Bertha. As a Christian, Bertha was naturally eager to convert her pagan husband. She therefore wrote to Pope Gregory the Great, who accordingly sent over St Augustine – then Prior of the monastery of St Andrew in Rome – to effect the conversion and refound the Church in England. Ethelbert gave Augustine a warmish welcome, but his initial response was guarded:

I see that you believe what you say, or you would not have come all this way to say it. But you must not expect me to renounce immediately the customs which I and the English have followed from one generation to another. So go on talking: no one will interfere with you and, if you convince us, of course it will follow that we will accept your message.

In the 1978 Cracker I included what I described as 'a nasty little bedtime story' by Victor Hugo, it went like this:
Bon Conseil aux Amants

Un brave ogre des bois, natif de Moscovie,
Etait fort amoureux d'une fée, et l'envie
Qu'il avait d'épouser cette dame s'accrut
Au point de rendre fou ce pauvre coeur tout brut.
L'ogre, un beau jour d'hiver, peigne sa peau velue,
Se présente au palais de la fée, et salue,
Et s'annonce à l'huissier comme prince Ogrousky.
La fée avait un fils, on ne sait pas de qui;
Elle était, ce jour-là, sortie, et quant au mioche,
Bel enfant blond, nourri de crème et de brioche,
Don fait par quelque Ulysse à cette Calypso,
It était sous la porte et jouait au cerceau.
On laissa l'ogre et lui tout seuls dans l'antichambre.
Comment passer le temps quand il neige, en décembre,
Et quand on n'a personne avec qui dire un mot?
L'ogre se mit alors à croquer le marmot.
C'est très simple. Pourtant c'est aller un peu vite,
Même lorsqu'on est ogre et qu'on est moscovite,
Que de gober ainsi les mioches du prochain.
Le bâillement d'un ogre est frère de la faim.
Quand la dame rentra, plus d'enfant; on s'informe.
Le fée avise l'ogre avec sa bouche énorme:
– As-tu vu, cria-t-elle, un bel enfant que j'ai?
Le bon ogre naif lui dit: Je l'ai mangé.
Or c'etait maladroit. Vous qui cherchez à plaire,
Ne mangez pas l'enfant dont vous aimez la mére.

I never got around to making a translation, but now I have found one. It is by Charles Sinker, whose mother has been kind enough to send me a copy. Alas, I have lost her letter, so have had no means of asking permission to make one very slight alteration, where the text seemed to me to depart a little too far from the original. For the rest, it's far better than I could ever have done.

Good Advice for Lovers

A worthy wood-ogre, near Moscow reared, was lovesick for a fairy; and he feared,

As the desire to wed this lady grew, that his poor brutish heart would break in two.

One fine cold day he combed his shaggy pelt and, coming to the palace where she dwelt,

Announced 'I'm Prince Ogrousky' to a groom. The fairy had a son, none knew by whom.

She had gone out that day; as for her son, a fair lad, fed on cream and sugar bun,

Some chance Ulysses' gift Calypso bore, he bowled his hoop beneath the palace door.

Ogre and boy were left alone together. How should one pass the time in snowy weather

With no one there with whom to have a chat? The ogre seized the child – and that was that.

It's all quite simple; still, a little much, even for ogres, Muscovites and such,

To wolf your neighbour's nippers at one bite. An ogre's yawn will match his appetite.

Madam returned. No child – a search took place. The fairy spied the ogre's gaping face:

'A lovely child of mine,' she cried, 'you met him?' 'Yes, ma'am', the honest ogre said, 'I ate him.'

Inept it was. If you would seem well-bred, don't eat the child whose mum you hope to wed.

Past Crackers have contained, over the years, a good many examples of atrocious verse. The series can easily be continued: Raymond Mortimer quotes, for example, in an essay on Tennyson (reprinted in his Try Anything Once *(1976) the following couplet, which was – it is only fair to say – omitted from the final draft of Tennyson's poem* Happy:

> I never glanced at her full bust but wished myself the snake
> That bit the harlot bosom of that heathen by the Nile

which might in turn be compared with Noel Coward's comment on a production of Antony and Cleopatra, *starring Dame Edith Evans at an age when she should have known better:*

> The greatest moment in the entire production was when the Asp advanced downstage and sobbed 'I can't go through with it . . .'

At Constantine, Cornwall, in the church of St Constantine, a wall slab commemorates one 'John Nicholas of Trebah', who died on the 27th of March 1788, aged 57:

> Here feeble nature drops the silent tear;
> While reason and religion, better taught,
> Congratulate the dead.

This provides, I think, an interesting contrast with an epitaph quoted by Robert Byron in First Russia then Tibet. *He attributes it to Sir Thomas Herbert, who apparently composed it at Jask on the Gulf of Oman, while accompanying Sir Dodmore Cotton and Sir Robert Shirley on an embassy to the King of Persia in 1627. (Later Herbert was Groom of the Bedchamber to Charles I and attended him on the scaffold.) It reads:*

> Here lies buried one Captain Shilling
> unfortunately slain by the insulting
> Portugall; but that his bones want
> sence and expression, they would tell
> you the earth is not worthy of his recep-
> tion, and that the people are blockish,
> rude, treacherous and indomitable.

On a Cat, Ageing

He blinks upon the hearth-rug,
And yawns in deep content,
Accepting all the comforts
That Providence has sent.

Loud he purrs and louder
In one glad hymn of praise
For all the night's adventures,
For quiet restful days.

Life will go on for ever,
With all that cat can wish,
Warmth and the glad procession
Of fish and milk and fish.

Only – the thought disturbs him –
He's noticed once or twice
The times are somehow breeding
A nimbler race of mice.

Alexander Gray

The sudden popularity of the 'Narnia' film has reminded me of Hugh Trevor-Roper's description of the book's author, in a letter to Professor Wallace Notestein:

Do you know C.S. Lewis? In case you don't, let me offer a brief character-sketch. Envisage (if you can) a man who combines the face and figure of a hog-reeve or earth-stopper with the mind and thoughts of a Desert Father of the fifth century, preoccupied with meditations of inelegant theological obscenity: a powerful mind warped by erudite philistinism, blackened by systematic bigotry, and directed by a positive detestation of such profane frivolities as art, literature and (of course) poetry: a purple-faced bachelor and misogynist, living alone in rooms of inconceivable hideousness, secretly consuming vast quantities of his favourite dish – beefsteak-and-kidney-pudding; periodically trembling at the mere apprehension of a feminine footfall; and all the while distilling his morbid and illiberal thoughts into volumes of best-selling prurient religiosity and such reactionary nihilism as is indicated by the gleeful title, *The Abolition of Man*. Such is C.S. Lewis, whom Magdalen College have now put up to recapture their lost monopoly of the chair of Poetry.

Horace Walpole on the founding of the British Museum. In 1753 he wrote to his friend Sir Horace Mann:

You will scarce guess how I occupy my time; chiefly at present in the guardianship of embryos and cockle-shells. Sir Hans Sloane is dead and has made me one of the Trustees to his Museum, which is to be offered for £20,000 to the King. He valued it at fourscore thousand; and so would anybody who loves hippopotamuses, sharks with one ear, and spiders as big as geese! It is a rent-charge to keep the foetuses in spirit! We are a charming wise set, all philosophers, botanists, antiquarians and mathematicians; and adjourned our first meeting because Lord Macclesfield, our chairman, was engaged to a party for finding out longitude. One of our number is a Moravian, who signs himself Henry XXVIII, Count de Reus. The Moravian has settled a colony at Chelsea, in Sir Hans's neighbourhood, and I believe he intended to beg Henry XXVIII's skeleton for his Museum.

Virginal exquisite queen, of long gentle thinking,
The colour of breaking day on a deserted sea.

Cynddelw Brydydd Mawr
(*'Cynddelw the Great Poet'*)
12th century
Tr. Glwn Williams

I am assured that the following is a true and faithful transcript of a radio conversation between U.S.S. Lincoln *and the Canadian authorities off the coast of Newfoundland. It was published in the* New York Times, *5 July 1998.*

Authorities: Please divert your course 15 degrees to the south to avoid a collision.

Lincoln: Recommend you divert your course 15 degrees to the north to avoid a collision.

Authorities: Negative. You will have to divert your course 15 degrees to the south to avert collision.

Lincoln: This is the Captain of the U.S. Navy ship. I say again, divert YOUR course.

Authorities: No. I say again, divert YOUR course.

Lincoln: THIS IS THE AIRCRAFT CARRIER U.S.S. LINCOLN, THE SECOND LARGEST SHIP IN THE UNITED STATES ATLANTIC FLEET. WE ARE ACCOMPANIED BY THREE DESTROYERS, THREE CRUISERS AND NUMEROUS ESCORT VESSELS. I DEMAND THAT YOU CHANGE YOUR COURSE 15 DEGREES NORTH. I SAY AGAIN, THAT IS ONE FIVE DEGREES NORTH, OR COUNTER-MEASURES WILL BE TAKEN TO ENSURE THE SAFETY OF THIS SHIP.

Authorities: This is a lighthouse. Your call.

BONUS

The Naval Chronicle, Volume XIV of 1805, included a translation of a contemporary French account of the Battle of Trafalgar. This was very kindly sent me by the Hon. Hugh Lawson, of the King George's Fund for Sailors. It is interestingly different to the sort of thing we are used to.

FIRST BULLETIN OF THE GRAND NAVAL ARMY

[From the MONITEUR, as it appeared in the HERALD.]

Head Quarters, Cadiz, Oct. 25

The operations of the Grand Naval Army second in the Atlantic those of the Grand Imperial Army in Germany. – The English fleet is annihilated! – Nelson is no more! Indignant at being inactive in port, whilst our brave brethren in arms were gaining laurels in Germany, Admirals Villeneuve and Gravina resolved to put to sea, and give the English battle. They were superior in number, forty-five to our thirty-three; but what is superiority in numbers to men determined to conquer? – Admiral Nelson did every thing to avoid a battle; he attempted to get into the Mediterranean, but we pursued, and came up with him off Trafalgar.

The French and Spaniards vied with each other who should first get into action. Admirals Villeneuve and Gravina were both anxious to lay their ships alongside the Victory, the English Admiral's ship. Fortune, so constant always to the Emperor, did not favour either of them – the *Santissima Trinidada* [sic] was the fortunate ship. In vain did the English Admiral try to evade an action: the Spanish Admiral Oliva prevented his escape, and lashed his vessel to the British Admiral. The English ship was one of 136 guns, the Santissima Trinidada was but a 74. – Lord Nelson adopted a new system: afraid of combating us in the old way, in which he knows we have a superiority of skill, as was proved by our victory over Sir Robert Calder, he attempted a new mode of fighting. For a short time they disconcerted us; but what can long disconcert his Imperial Majesty's arms? We fought yard-arm to yard-arm, gun to gun. Three hours did we fight in this manner: the English began to be dismayed – they found it impossible to resist us; but our brave sailors were tired of this slow means of gaining a victory; they wished to board; the cry was, '*à la bordage!*' [*sic*]. Their impetuosity was irresistible. At that moment two Ships, one French and one Spanish, boarded the *Téméraire*; the English fell back in astonishment and affright – we rushed to the flagstaff – struck the colours – and all were so anxious to be the bearer of the intelligence to their own ship, that they jumped overboard; and the English Ship, by this unfortunate impetuosity of our brave sailors and their allies, was able, by the assistance of two more Ships that came to her assistance, to make her escape in a sinking state.

Meanwhile Nelson still resisted us. It was now who should first board, and have the honour of taking him, French or Spaniard – two Admirals on each side disputed the honour – they boarded his Ship at the same moment – Villeneuve flew to the quarter-deck – with the usual generosity of the French, he carried a brace of pistols in his hands, for he knew the Admiral had lost his arm, and could not use his sword – he offered one to Nelson: they fought, and at the second fire Nelson fell; he was immediately carried below. Oliva, Gravina and Villeneuve attended him with the accustomed French humanity. – Meanwhile, fifteen of the English Ships of the line had struck – four more were obliged to follow their example – another blew up. Our victory was now complete, and we prepared to take possession of our prizes; but the elements were this time unfavourable to us; a dreadful storm came on – Gravina made his escape to his own Ship at the beginning of it – the Commander in Chief, Villeneuve and a Spanish Admiral were unable, and remained on board the Victory. – The storm was long and dreadful; our Ships being so well manoeuvred rode out the gale; the English, being so much more damaged, were driven ashore and many of them wrecked.

At length, when the gale abated, thirteen sail of the French and

Spanish line got safe to Cadiz; – the other twenty have, no doubt, gone to some other port, and will soon be heard of. We shall repair our damages as speedily as possible, go again in pursuit of the enemy, and afford them another proof of our determination to wrest from them the empire of the seas, and to comply with His Imperial Majesty's demand of Ships, Colonies and Commerce. Our loss was trifling, that of the English was immense. We have, however, to lament the absence of Admiral Villeneuve, whose ardour carried him beyond the strict bounds of prudence, and by compelling him to board the English Admiral's Ship, prevented him from returning to his own. After having acquired so decisive a victory, we wait with impatience the Emperor's order to sail to the enemy's shore, annihilate the rest of his navy, and thus complete the triumphant work we have so brilliantly begun.

A Christmas Cracker

2007

From an obituary notice in the Daily Telegraph, *November 2001*:

Melvin Burkhart, who has died aged 94, was a fairground sideshow performer known as the Human Blockhead because of his ability to drive a five-inch nail or an icepick into his head without flinching.

The Human Blockhead worked under a number of alternative titles, depending on which of his extraordinary repertoire of physical contortions he happened to be performing at the time.

As the Anatomical Wonder, he could inflate one lung at a time and dislocate his shoulders; as the Man without a Stomach, he could suck his stomach back to his spine; as the Two-Faced Man, he could frown with half his face and smile with the other half. Among many other accomplishments, he swallowed swords, threw knives and ate fire.

He was universally admired by his fellow performers, one of whom observed: 'Anyone who has ever hammered a five-inch nail into his nose owes a large debt to Melvin Burkhart.'

My Lady Gainsbourer meet us at Burley, but in sutch a dres as I never saw without disput. Her iengan manto is the worst of the kind, it is purpl, and a great dell of green, and a letel gould, and great flouers, ther is some red with the green, and noe lining, which looks most a bomenable.

Miss Bridget Noel, *in a letter to*
the Countess of Rutland, 1686.

Early in April 1903, A.C. Benson cycled to Putney, stopping at No.2 The Pines, an undistinguished semi-detached house of yellow brick with a tiny unkempt garden in front. It was the home of Algernon Charles Swinburne and his elderly companion Theodore Watts-Dunton. 'The house', Benson wrote in his diary, 'was redolent of cooking, dark, not very clean-looking, but comfortable enough – the walls crowded everywhere with pictures, mostly Rossetti's designs in pen and ink or chalk.' Watts-Dunton took him upstairs to a study above the dining-room.

There stood before me a little, pale, rather don-like man, quite bald, with a huge head and dome-like forehead, a ragged red beard in odd wisps – small aquiline red nose; he looked supremely shy, but received me with a distinguished courtesy, drumming on the ground with his foot and uttering strange little whistling noises.

. . . On the fender was a pair of brown socks. W.-D. said to me 'he has just come in from one of his long walks', took up the socks and put them behind a coal scuttle. 'Stay!' said Swinburne, and took them out carefully holding them in his hand, 'they are drying.' W.-D. murmured something to me about his fearing they would get scorched and we sate down. Swinburne sate down concealing his feet behind a chair and proceeded with strange motions to put the socks on out of sight. 'He seems to be changing them,' said W.-D. Swinburne said nothing but continued to whistle and drum. Then he rose and bowed me down to lunch.

This odd little story I found in On the Edge of Paradise: A.C. Benson, the Diarist, *by David Newsome. In 1903 Swinburne was sixty-six. There is another nice little story about him from the* Oxford Dictionary of National Biography:

In 1867 Rossetti decided to put Swinburne in the hands of 'some sensible young woman who would make a man of him'. He solicited the aid of Adah Isaacs Menken, a stage performer, to seduce him. Needless to say, the attempt failed, and Miss Menken returned the £10 fee to Rossetti as unearned. 'I can't make him understand,' she explained, 'that biting's no use!'

I ride the great black horses of my heart
With reins of steel across their flying hair;
So slow are they to halt, so swift to start,
The stormy-breasted stallions of despair.
Dark as the night and fretful as the air,
Fleeter than hounds that go with bellies thinned –
My wrists of all their strength have none to spare
When those black hunters lean upon the wind.
What if the sudden thunder of their feet
Wakes like a dream some farmer from his rest?
Dreams had I too, farmer, before these fleet
Steeds of the night had broken from their nest.
Their weary flanks are green and white with foam,
Sleep, brother, sleep; I bring my horses home.

Robert Nathan

The late Hugh, Thane of Cawdor, left behind a commonplace book, extracts of which were subsequently published under the title Thistles in Aspic. *I normally make a point of avoiding other people's anthologies, but I have made the occasional exception and I'm making another one now.*

Virginia Woolf on Edith Sitwell:

Transparent like some white bone one picks up on a moor, with sea water stones on her long frail hands which slide into yours, much narrower than one expects, like a folded fan.

Emerald, Lady Cunard on Lord Valentine Thynne:

So witty and handsome . . . one of the great lovers. Anne Islington adored him and Miss Winifred Barnes, the musical comedy actress, fell over a very small cliff for love of him.

Eric Linklater on Sir Compton Mackenzie:

He was two days unshaven, and his hair hung like a mother raven shot upon the nest. His clothes resembled the adjectives in a poem by Gerard Manley Hopkins: chosen for their texture and colour, and often most arbitrarily joined.

Some strangely refreshing information about Florence Nightingale, imparted by Jeremy Clarke in the Sunday Telegraph, *22 July 2001:*

> During the Crimean War, more soldiers died under her care at Scutari than in any of the front-line casualty stations. Of the three hundred Grenadier Guards she nursed during her first seven months there, not one survived.

(I was subsequently taken to task about this by Col. O.J.M. Lindsay, CBE, FRHistS, Editor of the 'Guards Magazine'. The colonel suggested that I might have based my statement on the Daily Telegraph *article – I had in fact said so at the start – and quoted another, by Algernon Percy, to the effect that 'Nightingale had not been running a hospital, she had been running a death camp.'*

Still, it is only fair to print his refutation: Hamilton's history of the Grenadiers states that 511 of all ranks died in hospitals in the Crimea, Turkey, Malta, Cyprus, England, at sea or elsewhere, while 755 other ranks recovered and returned to duty. It names some individuals who were invalided to Scutari in the late winter of early spring of 1855, when Florence was there, and then returned to England, sufficiently recovered.

A recent auction on E-bay ended with a pair of leather trousers being sold, after twenty-two bids, for $102.50. Prospective buyers may have been attracted by a short essay by the vendor:

You are bidding on a mistake. We all make mistakes. We date the wrong people for too long. We chew gum with our mouths open. We say inappropriate things in front of grandma.

And we buy leather pants.

I can explain those pants and why they are in my possession. I bought them many many years ago under the spell of a woman whom I believed to have taste. She suggested I try them on. I did. She said they looked good. I wanted to have a relationship of sorts with her. I'm stupid and prone to impulsive decisions. I bought the pants.

The relationship, probably for the better, never materialized. The girl, whose name I can't even recall, is a distant memory. I think she was short.

Ultimately, the pants were placed in the closet where they have remained, unworn, for nearly a decade. I would like to emphasize that aside from trying these pants on, they have never, ever, been worn. In public or private.

I have not worn these leather pants for a number of reasons:

I am not a member of Queen.
I do not like motorcycles.
I am not Rod Stewart.
I am not French.
I do not cruise for transvestites in an expensive sports car.

These were not cheap leather pants. They are Donna Karan leather pants. They're for men. Brave men, I would think. Perhaps tattooed, pierced men. In fact, I'll go so far as to say

251

you either have to be very tough, very gay or very famous to wear these pants and get away with it.

Again, they're men's pants, but they'd probably look great on the right lady. Ladies can get away with leather pants much more often than men can. It's a sad fact that men who own leather pants will have to come to terms with.

They are size 34 x 34. I am no longer size 34 x 34, so even were I to suddenly decide I was a famous gay biker I would not be able to wear these pants. These pants are destined for someone else. For reasons unknown – perhaps to keep my options open, in case I wanted to become a pirate – I have shuffled these unworn pants from house to house, closet to closet. Alas, it is now time to part ways so that I may use the extra room for any rhinestone-studded jeans I may purchase in the future.

These pants are in excellent condition. They were never taken on pirate expeditions. They weren't worn onstage. They didn't straddle a Harley, or a guy named Harley. They just hung there, sad and ignored, for a few presidencies.

Someone, somewhere, will look great in these pants. I'm hoping that someone is you, or that you can be suckered into buying them by a girl you're trying to bed. Please buy these leather pants.

Lady Salisbury asked me on one occasion to an intimate tea-party in Arlington Street, where the only other guests were Mr and Mrs Gladstone and Mr John Murray, grandson of the founder of the great publishing firm. Lord Salisbury, who was also present, sat apart with a grey Shetland shawl wound round his bearded face and shaggy head, the picture of silent misery. He had a bad toothache, it seemed. Mr Gladstone asked anxiously what he was doing about it. 'Nothing,' said Lord Salisbury. 'Nothing: hope it will pass.'

'But surely,' enquired Mr Gladstone, 'you've tried Butler's Nervine?'

No, Lord Salisbury had never even heard of it. Mr Gladstone at once proposed to go out and get some, and in spite of our attempts to stop him and send a servant, he bolted from the room and speedily returned in triumph with a bottle of the Nervine. Nor would he stop there. He insisted on applying the cure for himself. He made Lord Salisbury sit back in his chair and open his mouth. I watched Mr Gladstone peer into the open jaw of his great political adversary. The offending tooth was located, Mr Gladstone carefully applied cotton wool soaked in Nervine to the tender place. In five minutes Lord Salisbury had to own that the pain was gone, and he then, to my inexpressible relief, unwound the grey shawl from his enormous head.

Daisy, Countess of Warwick
Life's Ebb and Flow

It is a pity indeed that there was no Nervine in the days of Parson James Woodforde, who on Monday 24 October 1785 recorded in his diary:

The tooth-Ach so very bad all night and the same this morn' that I sent for John Reeves the Farrier who lives at the Hart and often draws Teeth for People, to draw one for me. He returned with my Man about 11 o'clock this Morning and he pulled it out for me the first Pull, but it was a monstrous Crash and more so, it being one of the Eye Teeth, it had but one Fang but that was very long. I gave Johnny Reeves for drawing it 0.2.6. A great pain in the Jaw Bone continued all Day and Night but nothing so bad as the Tooth Ach.

Early in 1866 Mr Gladstone, as Chancellor of the Exchequer, moved a resolution for the payment of £6,000 a year to Princess Helena on her marriage with Prince Christian of Schleswig-Holstein. This prompted the following letter to The Times, *which appeared on 24 February:*

Sir,

Being myself a mother, although I do not wish to speak severe of Mr Gladstone, as would be ungrateful in one of a class has to thank him in regard of tea and sugar, still, truth is truth, and having read in The Times daily newspaper today that he should say Princess Helena were the eldest unmarried daughter at the time of the demise of the great and good Prince Consort, beg to say that if you will look in Dod's Peerage, which one of my lodgers have left here, but not the rent, will see that the late Prince's loss occurred 14 December, 1861, and that the dear Princess Alice Maud Mary, whose conduct at the time was generally spoke of admiration and love, were married 1st July, 1862, and I think that right is right, but remain

Your obedient servant,
M. MIGGS

Bouverie-street, Feb.23.

(Thanks, John Parker.)

Three passions, simple but overwhelmingly strong, have governed my life: the longing for love, the search for knowledge, and unbearable pity for the suffering of mankind. These passions, like great winds, have blown me hither and thither, in a wayward course over a deep ocean of anguish, reaching to the very verge of despair.

I have sought love, first, because it brings ecstasy – ecstasy so great that I would often have sacrificed all the rest of my life for a few hours of this joy. I have sought it next, because it relieves loneliness – that terrible loneliness in which one shivering consciousness looks over the rim of the world into the cold unfathomable lifeless abyss. I have sought it finally, because in the union of love I have seen, in a mystic miniature, the prefiguring vision of the heaven that saints and poets have imagined. This is what I have sought, and though it might seem too good for human life, this is what – at last – I have found.

With equal passion I have sought knowledge. I have wished to understand the hearts of men. I have wished to know why the stars shine. And I have tried to apprehend the Pythagorean power by which number holds sway above the flux. A little of this, but not much, I have achieved.

Love and knowledge, so far as they were possible, led upwards towards the heavens. But always pity brought me down to earth. Echoes and cries of pain reverberate in my heart. Children in famine, victims tortured by oppressors, helpless old people a hated burden to their sons, and the whole world of loneliness, poverty and pain make a mockery of what human life should be. I long to alleviate the evil, but I cannot, and I too suffer.

This has been my life. I have found it worth living and would gladly live it again if the chance were offered me.

Bertrand Russell

Elsewhere, he writes:

An individual human existence should be like a river – small at first, narrowly contained within its banks, and rushing passionately past boulders and over waterfalls. Gradually the river grows wider, the banks recede, the waters flow more quietly, and in the end, without any visible break, they become merged in the sea and painlessly lose their individual being. The man who, in old age, can see his life in this way will not suffer from the fear of death, since the things he cares for will continue.

My dear friend Hector McDonnell calls my attention to The Cambridge English-Hindi Romanised Dictionary (Pankaj Publications, New Delhi, 1977). It includes the following phrases for a railway journey:

Which is my seat?
Where is the reservation office?
I want a seat reserved.
We do the reservation only ten days before the journey
The train is very crowded
There is much noise
People are pushing one another
The compartment is very hot
Some are using abusive language
The fan is not working
The lavatory is very dirty
There is no water in the lavatory
The compartment is full of flies

Hurry up
Get into the compartment
The engine is whistling
The Guard is waving the green flag
But there is no room in the compartment
Every seat is occupied
Try the next compartment
There the condition is much worse
The train is moving
Don't jump. Don't take the risk.

Another dear friend, Nina Lobanov has sent me a cutting from the Edinburgh Evening News, *18 August 1978*:

> While they were waiting at a bus stop in Clermiston, Mr and Mrs Daniel Thirsty were threatened by Mr Robert Clear. 'He demanded that I give him my wife's purse', said Mr Thirsty. 'Telling him that the purse was in her basket, I bent down, put my hands up her skirt, detached her artificial leg and hit him over the head with it. It was not my intention to do anything more than frighten him off, but, unhappily for us all, he died.'

I am tempted to think that the names of Shakespeare's children were not chosen arbitrarily or sentimentally, though the evidence suggests otherwise. Hamnet and Judith were, we are told, named for Master and Mistress Sadler, who were neighbours of the Shakespeares. Susanna is just a good, rather Puritanical, biblical name. But Susanna also stands as a symbol of purity assailed by the lust of elders. In later years, when Susanna Shakespeare became Susanna Hall, wife of a respected local doctor, she repudiated a charge of adultery and saw her accuser excommunicated. In babyhood her name was ironical; she was the product of lust, not love, and there was one lustful elder involved, Anne Hathaway. When Will chose the name Holofernes for the pedantic pedagogue of *Love's Labour's Lost,* he took it from the pedantic tutor of Gargantua in Rabelais. Gargantua is mentioned in *As You Like It;* Shakespeare knew his Rabelais (further proof comes in Dr Hotson's discussion of the provenance of the 'Vapians' in *Twelfth Night).* Had Rogers, town clerk of Stratford, been teaching Will French as a language necessary for the law, and had he been using Rabelais as a text? Did Will, remembering that he had been a sort of Holofernes himself, start thinking of the first Holofernes and the woman associated with him? He had now a child whose name began with an S, and another whose name was to begin with a J, and, with Stratford perhaps deluged by the late January or early February rains, he might see himself as a sort of Noah, the names of whose children began respectively with an S and a J and, finally, an H. He could not have a Shem or a Japhet but he could have a Ham, or rather a little Ham. Hamnet was the common diminutive, and frequently found in those days both as a first name and as a patronymic. A Kate Hamnet had, during Will's boyhood, drowned herself in the Avon – some said for love. Ophelia, maddened by the death of a father she loved, was also to drown herself. Hamlet and Hamnet were interchangeable. The provincial English mouth found the consonant group *mn* difficult to pronounce and preferred to say *chimley* for *chimney,* often interposing the buffer of a *b* between the nasal and the lateral. We still hear *chimbley.* Young Hamnet Shakespeare probably heard 'Hamblet!' when he was wanted for supper or bed. The whole of this paragraph is very unsound.

Anthony Burgess, *Shakespeare (1970)*

On a visit earlier this year to Galapagos we encountered a giant tortoise called Lonesome George and were treated to a long disquisition on his extremely unsatisfactory sex life. He was believed to be 150 years old or even more. I suddenly remembered an observation by the great naturalist Gilbert White of Selborne:

It is a matter of wonder that Providence should bestow such a profusion of days and such seeming waste of longevity on a reptile that appears to relish it so little.

From an Exeter newspaper. Alas, I have lost the cutting since I copied it out, so cannot give the exact date:

Donna Challice, a thirty-year-old single mother of three from Devon, has appeared in court accused of failing properly to recycle her household waste. Mrs Challice was being prosecuted for 'contaminating recyclable rubbish' under the Environmental Protection Act. She has now been released on bail and will next appear on 5 June 2006 for a pre-trial review.

The Environmental Protection Act specifically states which types of recyclable items must be cleaned and placed in which containers on which days. Mrs Challice has been accused of putting items in the wrong bins on six separate occasions over the last year. She claims that the rules are confusing and that any offence that she may have committed was completely by accident.

Arthur Dimson, Director of Waste Disposal for the Exeter City Council, has dismissed Mrs Challice's claim, saying that:

'It's quite simple really. On the second and fourth Monday of each month, plastics go in the red bins and aluminium in the blue bins. On the first and third Tuesdays of each month – providing there has already been a first Monday – paper goes into the red containers and other non-aluminium metals go in the blue containers. If there hasn't been a first Monday, the schedule is pushed back a week. On alternating Wednesdays, glass goes into the red cans and miscellaneous recyclable refuse goes into the blue cans. On Thursdays, nonrecyclable refuse may be put into either the red or the blue receptacles. All discards must be washed except clothing – which may be either washed or drycleaned depending on the fabric – and paper. Paper with coloured printing should only be placed in the red cans on the first Tuesday of each month. Paper with only black ink may be placed in the red containers on any other qualifying Tuesday. On weekends the bins are to remain empty for cleaning. These rules are all posted on the bottom of each recycling bin. So it's not as if people have to memorise them.'

He added:

'Mrs Challice could wait until the weekend and look in the bottom of the empty bin to refresh her memory on the rules.'

George Koltanowski died on 5 February 2000, aged ninety-six. Here is an abridgement of his obituary in The Times:

George Koltanowski made his mark on the world of chess by virtue not so much of his playing strength (though he was made an honorary grandmaster in 1988) as for his extraordinary memory, which enabled him to play a large number of games simultaneously without sight of the board. He could also conduct a blindfold 'knight's tour', in which a chess knight covers the whole board using legal moves but using each square only once.

Koltanowski embellished such public performances with curious extra details, such as performing the feat over three boards or writing additional information on the squares. An eyewitness reported of one such display: 'Koltanowski has given the puzzle a spectacular twist: he fills in the squares with names, phone numbers, banknote serial numbers and the like, given him by the audience. He then takes a few minutes (often less than three) completely to memorise the board, and then does the knight's tour by hopping from one item to another. 'I'll go from Paris to San Francisco, to 673 3869 to 234 89 0768' and so forth. He has even gone one step further and completed a knight's tour on a board he had not seen for a year.

His true ambition was in the world of blindfold chess. In 1931 he set up a world record by scoring 25 points from a possible 30 in an exhibition at Antwerp. Over two and a half hours, without sight of any of the boards, he won 20 games and drew 10. He bettered even this in Edinburgh in 1937, completing 34 games in 13½ hours. Again he lost no games, drawing 10 and winning 24...

Even in his fifties Koltanowski continued to set up world records in the realm of blindfold play. In December 1960 he played against 56 opponents consecutively at the rate of 10 seconds a move over 9¾ hours. Amazingly, he conducted the entire display blindfold, and once again he did not lose a single game, winning 50 and drawing 6.

I have often observed that for the greater part of my life I have been trying to make myself ill, and then, when I had achieved this, in trying to get well again. I have been equally successful in both; and now that, as far as that goes, I enjoy perfect health, I regret being unable to make myself ill; but old age, an illness as cruel as it is inevitable, forces me to be well in spite of myself.

Casanova

A few choice analogies and metaphors found in school compositions:

Her face was a perfect oval, like a circle that had its sides gently compressed by a Thigh Master.

He spoke with the wisdom that can only come from experience, like a guy who went blind from a solar eclipse without one of those boxes with a pinhole in it and now goes around the country speaking at high schools about the dangers of looking at a solar eclipse without one of those boxes with a pinhole in it.

John and Mary had never met. They were like two hummingbirds who had also never met.

Shots rang out, as shots are wont to do.

The young fighter had a hungry look, the kind you get from not eating for a while.

He was as lame as a duck. Not the metaphorical lame duck, either, but a real duck that was actually lame, maybe from stepping on a land mine or something.

Though it may be unessential to the imagination, travel is necessary to an understanding of men. Only with long experience and the opening of his wares on many a beach where his language is not spoken, will the merchant come to know the worth of what he carries, and what is parochial and what is universal in his choice. Such delicate goods as justice, love and honour, courtesy, and indeed all the things we care for, are valid everywhere; but they are variously moulded and often differently handled, and sometimes nearly unrecognizable if you meet them in a foreign land; and the art of learning fundamental common values is perhaps the greatest gain of travel to those who wish to live at ease among their fellows.

Freya Stark,
Perseus in the Wind

In 2003 the Orchestra of the Age of Enlightenment made a concert tour of Japan with the violinist Viktoria Mullova. The fourth city to be visited was Choshi. Here is the text, very slightly abridged, of the Mayor's speech of welcome, delivered in English.

Dearest Madam Mullova, honourable members of the Orchestra of the Age of Enlightenment, beautifully aged and beloved musical instruments, ladies and gentlemen:

All welcome to the city of Choshi. I really appreciate that Choshi city was chosen in O.A.E. Japan-tour as fourth programme place I was really proud when I found the familiar name of Choshi city printed on the beautiful programmes, along with such big names as Sapporo, Yokohama and Tokyo.

Since I began my career in Mayor's office last year, I tried to construct 'a City of Culture and Education'. I eagerly promised various citizen involvement programmes to stir up brilliant breezes of art and culture and also to improve economic amenity of citizen life . . . It is my greatest pleasure, not only as Mayor, but also as one of art-loving citizens, to have opportunity of fragrant music-concert performed and perfumed here in a small local city, a little bit different from Glyndebourne, by the world-famous violinist and Leader Mackintosh's colleagues' ultra-super orchestra. I am looking forward to tomorrow concert very much, because I have a strong and prolonged reason in season. Please forgive me to boast a little bit. Tomorrow night performance is my third experience. Nine years ago or so, first encounter with O.A.E. Orchestra in West Germany. I did not even know the meaning of the strange name of the Orchestra. I took that it had something to do with lighter or burning-out show. Secondly, this time, three nights ago, I was wise enough to drive three hours to Yokohama. Both nights, all sounds were perfectly controlled and pleasantly warm with mostly Mozart-like flavour.

I planned tonight party to express our citizens' sincerest

thanks. I hope that multi-lateral intercourse will occur among artists and citizens, men and music, I give happiest worship to four angels of music, who are jealous Salieri, frank Schubert, wolfgangster Mozart and, fourthly, miraculously victorious Madam Mullova. I express my thanks to all attending the party, including luckiest students who have just learned through the heavy lessons this afternoon, that 'work-shop' truly means sweaty and laborious 'warship' or 'wor-ship'.

My dear staff prepared entertainment programmes of Japanese traditional dances, Japanese harp-and-bamboo-recorder ensemble concert, and short programme by some of those just-reborn students' 'frightenment-orchestra'.

In the Tatami Room, Tea Ceremony is to be held. Chairs are served, don't be afraid. Please see-and-try Japanese traditional tastes. Enlighten yourselves to be burntout. Thank you. Thank you very much.

From the Society of Editors Newsletter (Australia), Vol. 24, No.2 (September 1994)

A motion was tabled the other day at the Professional Association of Teachers Conference in Cheltenham, England:

'This conference believes that *mens sana in corpore sano* should in 1994 read *men's and women's sana in corpore sano.*'

'The motion was put forward by members of the independent schools section', explained General Secretary John Andrews. 'I would hope they knew what the original phrase meant . . . but I'm not sure.'

In the little church of Fenstanton in Cambridgeshire – it was in Huntingdonshire until that sad day in 1972 when they unforgivably redrew the county map of England – stands the tomb of Capability Brown. The epitaph reads:

Ye sons of elegance, who truly taste
The Simple charms that genuine Art supplies,
Come from the sylvan Scenes His Genius grac'd,
And offer here your tributary Sighs.
But know that more than Genius slumbers here;
Virtues were his which Art's best powers transcend.
Come, ye Superior train, who these revere,
And weep the Christian, Husband, Father, Friend.

Humphry Repton, on the other hand, was buried in the churchyard at Aylsham, Norfolk. He wrote his own epitaph:

Not like the Egyptian tyrants consecrate,
Unmixed with others shall my dust remain;
But mold'ring, blending, melting into Earth,
Mine shall give form and colour to the Rose,
And while its vivid blossoms cheer mankind,
Its perfumed odours shall ascend to Heaven.

'Our outlook is totally different from that of our American cousins, who have never had an aristocracy. Americans relate all effort, all work and all of life itself to the dollar. Their talk is of nothing but dollars. The English seldom sit happily chatting for hours on end about pounds.'

Nancy Mitford, *Noblesse Oblige*

This provoked the following open letter from Ogden Nash:

MS FOUND UNDER A SERVIETTE IN A LOVELY HOME

Dear Cousin Nancy:
    You probably never heard of me or Cousin Beauregard or Cousin Yancey,
    But since you're claiming kin all the way across the ocean, we figure you must be at least partwise Southern,
    So we consider you not only our kith and kin but also our kithin' couthern.
    I want to tell you, when Cousin Emmy Lou showed us your piece it stopped the conversation flat,
    Because I had twenty dollars I wanted to talk about, and Cousin Beauregard had ten dollars he wanted to talk about, and Cousin Yancey didn't have any dollars at all, and he wanted to talk about that.
    But Cousin Emmy Lou looked over her spectacles, which the common people call glasses,
    And she offered us a dollar to stop talking about dollars and start talking about the English upper classes.
    Cousin Beauregard wanted to know why the English aristocracy was called English when most of their names were French to begin with,
    And now anybody with an English name like Hobbs or Stobbs

has to accumulate several millions of those pounds they seldom chat about, to buy his way in with.

Cousin Yancey said he could understand that – the St Aubyns beat the hell out of the Hobbses in 1066 – but there was a more important point that he could not determine,

Which is why the really aristocratic English aristocrats have names that are translated from the German.

Cousin Emmy Lou is pretty aristocratic herself; in spite of her weakness for hog jowl and potlikker, she is noted for her highborn pale and wan flesh,

And where most people get gooseflesh she gets swanflesh,

And she said she thought you ought to know that she had been over the royal roster

And she had spotted at least one imposter.

She noticed that the Wicked Queen said 'mirror, mirror on the wall' instead of 'looking-glass, looking-glass on the wall', which is perfectly true,

So the Wicked Queen exposed herself as not only wicked but definitely non-U.

We finally agreed with you that the English aristocracy have a tough row to hoe, but it has one spectacular solace:

Where there is unrest overseas and all other envoys have failed, it can call on a charming royal personage, whereas we can only offer John Foster Dulles.

After that, we all loosened our collars

And resumed our conversation about dollars.

For there is no medicine for love, neither meat, nor drink, nor any charm, but only kissing and embracing, and lying naked together.

Longus: *Daphnis and Chloe.*
Tr. George Thornley, 1657

BONUS

A Time of Gifts – the first volume of Paddy Leigh Fermor's alas unfinished account of his great walk, while still in his teens, from the Channel to Constantinople – is, as might be expected, a tour de force. Here is one of its great set pieces: his description of the Hofbräuhaus, the famous Munich beer-cellar:

I was back in beer-territory. Halfway up the vaulted stairs a groaning Brownshirt, propped against the wall on a swastika'd arm, was unloosing, in a staunchless gush down the steps, the intake of hours. Love's labour lost. Each new storey radiated great halls given over to ingestion. In one chamber a table of S.A. men were grinding out *Lore, Lore, Lore* scanning the slow beat with the butts of their mugs, then running the syllables in double time, like the carriages of an express: 'UND – KOMMT – DER – FRUHlingindastal! GRUSS – MIR – DIE – LORenocheinmal'. But it was certain civilian figures seated at meat that drew the glance and held it.

One must travel east for a hundred and eighty miles from the Upper Rhine and seventy north from the Alpine watershed to form an idea of the transformation that beer, in collusion with almost nonstop eating – meals within meals dovetailing so closely during the hours of waking that there is hardly an interprandial moment – can wreak on the human frame. Intestine strife and the truceless clash of intake and digestion wrecks many German tempers, twists brows into scowls and breaks out in harsh words and deeds.

The trunks of these feasting burghers were as wide as casks. The spread of their buttocks over the oak benches was not far short of a yard. They branched at the loins into thighs as thick as the torsos of ten-year-olds and arms on the same scale strained

275

like bolsters at the confining serge. Chin and chest formed a single column, and each close-packed nape was creased with its three deceptive smiles. Every bristle had been cropped and shaven from their knobbly scalps. Except when five o'clock veiled them with shadow, surfaces as polished as ostriches' eggs reflected the lamplight. The frizzy hair of their wives was wrenched up from scarlet necks and pinned under slides and then hatted with green Bavarian trilbys and round one pair of elephantine shoulders a little fox stole was clasped. The youngest of this group, resembling a matinée idol under some cruel spell, was the bulkiest. Under tumbling blond curls his china blue eyes protruded from cheeks that might have been blown up with a bicycle pump, and cherry lips laid bare the sort of teeth that make children squeal. There was nothing bleary or stunned about their eyes. The setting may have reduced their size, but it keyed their glances to a sharper focus. Hands like bundles of sausages flew nimbly, packing in forkload on forkload of ham, salami, frankfurter, krenwurst and blutwurst and stone tankards were lifted for long swallows of liquid which sprang out again instantaneously on cheek and brow. They might have been competing with stop-watches, and their voices, only partly gagged by the cheekfuls of good things they were grinding down, grew louder while their unmodulated laughter jarred the air in frequent claps. Pumpernickel and aniseed rolls and bretzels [sic] bridged all the slack moments but supplies always came through before a true lull threatened. Huge oval dishes, laden with schweinebraten, potatoes, sauerkraut, red cabbage and dumplings were laid in front of each diner. They were followed by colossal joints of meat – unclassifiable helpings which, when they were picked clean, shone on the scoured chargers like calves' pelvises or the bones of elephants. Waitresses with the build of weight-lifters and all-in wrestlers whirled this provender along and features dripped and glittered like faces at an ogre's banquet. But all too soon the table was an empty bone-yard once more, sound faltered, a look of bereavement clouded those small eyes and there was a brief hint of sorrow in the air. But succour was always at hand; beldames barged to the rescue at full gallop with new clutches of mugs and fresh plate-loads of consumer goods; and the damp Laestrygonian brows unpuckered again in a happy renewal of clamour and intake.

I strayed by mistake into a room full of S.S. officers, Gruppen- and Sturmbannführers, black from their lightning-flash collars to the forest of tall boots underneath the table. The window embrasure was piled high with their skull-and-crossbones caps. I still hadn't found the part of this Bastille I was seeking, but at last a noise like the rush of a river guided me downstairs again to my journey's end.

The vaults of the great chamber faded into infinity through blue strata of smoke. Hobnails grated, mugs clashed and the combined smell of beer and bodies and old clothes and farmyards sprang at the newcomer. I squeezed in at a table full of peasants, and was soon lifting one of those masskrugs to my lips. It was heavier than a brace of iron dumb-bells, but the blond beer inside was cool and marvellous, a brooding, cylindrical litre of Teutonic myth. This was the fuel that had turned the berserk feeders upstairs into Zeppelins and floated them so far from heart's desire. The gunmetal-coloured cylinders were stamped with a blue HB conjoined under the Bavarian crown, like the foundry-mark on cannon. The tables, in my mind's eye, were becoming batteries where each gunner served a silent and recoil-less piece of ordnance which, trained on himself, pounded away in a steady siege. *Mass*-gunfire! Here and there on the tables, with their heads in puddles of beer, isolated bombardiers had been mown down in their emplacements. The vaults reverberated with the thunder of a creeping barrage. There must have been over a thousand pieces engaged! – Big Berthas, Krupp's pale brood, battery on battery crashing at random or in salvoes as hands adjusted the elevation and traverse and then tightened on the stone trigger-guard. Supported by comrades, the walking wounded reeled through the battle smoke and a fresh gunner leaped into each place as it fell empty.

My own gun had fired its last shot, and I wanted to change to a darker-hued explosive. A new *Mass* was soon banged down on the board. In harmony with its colour, it struck a darker note at once, a long Wagnerian chord of black-letter semibreves: *Nacht und Nebel*! Rolling Bavarian acres formed on the inscape of the mind, fanning out in vistas of poles planted pyramidally with hope gadding over them heavy with poppy-sombre flowers.

The peasants and farmers and the Munich artisans that filled the tables were much nicer than the civic swallowers overhead. Compared to the trim, drilled figures of the few soldiers there, the Storm Troopers looked like brown-paper parcels badly tied with string. There was even a sailor with two black silk streamers falling over his collar from the back of his cap, round the front of which, in gold letters, was written *Unterseeboot*. What was this Hanseatic submariner doing here, so far inland from Kiel and the Baltic? My tablemates were from the country, big, horny-handed men, with a wife or two among them. Some of the older men wore green and grey loden jackets with bone buttons and badgers' brushes or blackcocks' feathers in the back of their hatbands. The bone mouthpieces of long cherrywood pipes were lost in their whiskers and on their glazed china bowls, painted castles and pine-glades and chamois glowed cheerfully while shag-smoke poured through the perforations of their metal lids. Some of them, gnarled and mummified, puffed at cheroots through which straws were threaded to make them draw better. They gave me one and I added a choking tribute to the enveloping cloud. The accent had changed again, and I could only grasp the meaning of the simplest sentences. Many words were docked of their final consonants; '*Bursch*' – 'a chap' – for instance, became 'bua'; 'A' was rolled over into 'O', 'O' became 'E', and every O and U seemed to have a final A appended, turning it into a dissyllable. All this set up a universal moo-ing note, wildly distorted by resonance and echo; for these millions of vowels, prolonged and bent into boomerangs, sailed ricochetting up through the fog to swell the tidal thunder. This echoing and fluid feeling, the bouncing of sounds and syllables and the hogsheads of pungent liquid that sloshed about the tables and blotted the sawdust underfoot, must have been responsible for the name of this enormous hall. It was called the *Schwemme*, or horse-pond. The hollowness of those tall mugs augmented the volume of noise like the amphorae which the Greeks embedded in masonry to add resonance to their chants. My own note, as the mug emptied, was sliding down to middle C.

Mammoth columns were rooted in the flagstones and the sawdust. Arches flew in broad hoops from capital to capital; crossing in diagonals, they groined the barrel-vaults that hung dimly above the smoke. The place should have been lit by pine-torches in stanchions. It was beginning to change, turning now, under my clouding glance, into the scenery for some terrible Germanic saga, where snow vanished under the breath of dragons whose red-hot blood thawed sword-blades like icicles. It was a place for battle-axes and bloodshed and the last pages of the *Nibelungenlied* when the capital of Hunland is in flames and everybody in the castle is hacked to bits. Things grew quickly darker and more fluid; the echo, the splash, the boom and the roar of fast currents sunk this beer-hall under the Rhine-bed; it became a cavern full of more dragons. misshapen guardians of gross treasure; or the fearful abode, perhaps, where Beowulf, after tearing the Grendel's arm out of its socket, tracked him over the snow by the bloodstains and, reaching the mere's edge, dived in to swim many fathoms down and slay his loathsome water-hog of a mother in darkening spirals of gore.

Or so it seemed, when the third mug arrived.

A
Christmas
Cracker

2008

Wilton's, the last surviving Victorian Music Hall in London, has been saved in the nick of time. After more than a century as a Methodist mission, it is now once again open for business. The following is taken from East London Sketches of Christian Work and Workers *by Thomas Walker, published in 1896.*

Four years before the Wesleyan Mission took the premises, Mrs Reginald Radcliffe and Miss Macpherson were passing through Grace's Alley into Wellclose Square as the evening performances in the music hall were proceeding. The dreadful hubbub that came from the hall startled them. They paused to listen, and were so impressed that they paid the admission fee and went in to see really what could be going on. The sights on the stage and the entire condition of things became so awful to them, that they fell down on their knees together, in the centre of the hall, and in view of the stage and the crowd of onlookers, prayed that God would break the power of the devil in the place, and bring the premises into the use of Christian people. Soon after this the place was closed, and the licences lapsed. It was not again opened until February 2, 1888, when it was opened in the name of Christ and His glory.

The Scandinavian Book, *by my old friend Peter Tennant, furnishes the following extracts from Ifvar Kraak's English Grammar for Swedes, published in 1748:*

You are a lazy body – *J ären en later sjusafware.*

If you want rise, I'll pull off your bed cloaths – *Om J intet wil stiga up, wil jag draga af edra sängteläder.*

Do you dress yourself in bed? Why, that's the fashion, sir – *Kläden j pa eder i sängen? Hurn da, det är sa bruket.*

Where is the wash ball? *Hwar är tval kulan?*

Why don't you button your waistcoat? I love to go open breast – *Hwarföre knäppen j intet till eder wäst? Jag tycker om at ga öpen i bröstet.*

Undress me – *Kläd af mig.*

Sweetheart, have you put on clean sheets? *Hör fästmö, han j lagt rena lakan pa?*

Where is the house of office, the little house, the chamber pot? – *Hwar är privetet, lillehuset, natt-pattan?*

Let's fetch a walk – *Lat oss göra en promenade.*

I hope the letting of blood will do you good – *Jag hoppas aderlatningen lär göra er godt.*

I am dying. Cheer up, be not cast down for so small a matter – *Jag lär dö. Frisk up, tappa intet modet för sa litet.*

He is in a consumption. Tis incurable disease. If asses milk does not cure him, nothing will – *Han har twinsot. Det är en obotelig sjukdom. Om asne-mjölk intet cureran honom, sa han intet hjelpa.*

I have but a puny stomach – *Jag har en dalig maga.*

What will you drink? Anything that's wet – *Hwed wiljen J dricka? Lika myeket, bara det är watt.*

I am almost fuddled – *Jag är nästan drucken.*

Since there's no helpe, Come let us kisse and part.
Nay, I have done. You get no more of Me,
And I am glad, yea glad with all my heart,
That thus so cleanly, I my Selfe can free.
Shake hands for ever, Cancell all our Vowes,
And when we meet at any time againe,
Be it not seene in either of our Browes
That We one jot of former Love reteyne;
Now at the last gaspe of Love's latest Breath,
When his Pulse fayling, Passion speechlesse lies,
When Faith is kneeling by his bed of Death,
And Innocence is closing up his Eyes,
Now if thou would'st, when all have given him over,
From Death to Life, thou might'st him yet recover.

Michael Drayton
(1563-1631)

Drayton was, like Shakespeare, a Warwickshire man, and almost exactly the same age – though he outlived Shakespeare by sixteen years. In my schooldays we all had to learn his famous poem on the Battle of Agincourt – 'Fair stood the wind for France' was its first and best line – but much of his work seems to me insufferably turgid. This sonnet is surely by far the greatest thing he ever wrote – one of the loveliest short poems in the language.

On 19 October 1941 Leopold Stokowski had conducted the César Franck Symphony with the New York Philharmonic Orchestra. Arturo Toscanini heard the performance on the radio and took up his pen:

My dear Stokowsky

This afternoon you have vitrolized Franck's Symphony . . . Never in my long life I have heard such a brutal, bestial, ignobil, unmusical performance like yours – not even from you.

The Divine Art of Music too, has its own ganster like Hitler and Mussolini . . . Believe me, you are ready for mad-house or for jail . . . Hurry up!

Toscanini

My friend Lois de Menil sends me the following dicta of former Vice-President Al Gore:

If we don't succeed, we run the risk of failure.

Welcome to President Clinton, Mrs Clinton and my fellow astronauts.

I believe we are on an irreversible trend towards more freedom and democracy – but that could change.

I have made good judgements in the past. I have made good judgements in the future.

The future will be better tomorrow.

I stand by all the misstatements that I've made. (August 17 1993)

A low voter turnout is an indication of fewer people going to the polls.

Illegitimacy is something we should talk about in terms of not having it. (May 20 1996)

We are ready for any unforeseen event that may or may not occur.

For NASA, space is still a high priority.

Quite frankly, teachers are the only profession that teach our children.

It isn't pollution that's harming the environment. It's the impurities in the air and water that are doing it.

It's time for the human race to enter the solar system.

I love wine; but I have always known that other people find dimensions in it to which I shall ever be blind. In my 1972 Cracker I included a couple of extracts from a wine catalogue of Gerald Asher ('just the wine for those who like the smell of Verdi'); but even he cannot match P. Morton Shand; the following is taken from A Book of French Wines, *published in 1928:*

Bordeaux, which was first belauded by Ausonius, has been called 'austere' and again 'un gentleman par excellence, le vin d'une correction impeccable'. Maurice des Ombiaux defines it as a wine of perfect scansion and rhythm, evocative of the polished verse of Racine and La Fontaine. To compare the magnificent harmony of a fine Bordeaux to a flight of Alexandrines is to pay it a doubtful compliment – outside of France at least – for the genius of no great wine is less emphatic, declamatory or monotonous. Grandeur it has, and in high degree, but I find the 'scansion' of Bordeaux, if scansion there must be, ranges from the Horatian to the Miltonic, from the rippling lyrics of Herrick to the sonorous sway and surge of Swinburne in the infinite variety of its scope; the 'rhythm' of its incarnadine burden, the lilt of splendid majesty, never the din of rant drowning the creaking of the buskins. It is a wine of superb carriage, of gracious manners, but its charms, as its virtues, are wholly feminine. Bordeaux is a great lady, not a *Grand Seigneur* . . .

A quoi bon fuir le parallèle
Avec un loyal ennemi?
Disons que le Bordeaux c'est 'Elle',
Et que le Bourgogne c'est 'Lui'.

On the following page he writes:

Tovey, writing in 1862, gravely recommends 'good, sound claret' as 'an agreeable substitute for tea or coffee at breakfast during warm weather', and suggests 'a ration of half a bottle for patriotic Riflemen after their early morning drills'.

I've had a little trouble with Tovey, but have eventually run him to earth on the internet. He is Charles Tovey, author of 'Wine and Wine Countries: A Record and Manual for Wine Merchants and Consumers'. *The first edition is indeed dated 1862.*

From the Winston-Salem Journal, *May 19, 2001:*

EDITH DOUB KIGER

November 26,1918 – May 12, 2001

The landscape of mother's life was simple. Mother was an ordinary person who lived an ordinary life; she had that quality called character – that is 'doing the right thing when no one is looking'. Mother always did the right thing at the right time for the right reason throughout her life. That was extraordinary.

Mother's actions exemplified the essence of a true Christian. She was unselfish, honest, loyal to her friends, polite to strangers and always put her family before herself.

Her pleasures were simple, her spirit caring. Her greatest internal pleasure was to love and be loved. Her greatest external pleasure was her beloved home and backyard: oaks, maples, leaves, ferns, clematis, camellias, leaves, azaleas, geraniums, leaves, petunias, periwinkles, marigolds, leaves, irises, hydrangeas, rhododendrons, dogwoods, leaves, leaves, leaves. Mulch, water, rake, haul, sweat. Early to bed, early to rise, work like mad and fertilize.

However, Edith Kiger, Guardian, Defender and Protector of 2630 Reynolds Road, had one failed cause. For 42 years she fearlessly, relentlessly, waged war on legions of squirrels, opossums, garter snakes, and battalions of rabbits, mice, voles and chipmunks. Now she won many skirmishes with these perky invaders and a few battles, but the Great War with Woodland Critters she lost. That enchanted backyard was their home too. So today we honor Mother's life and memory, and we give pause to the generations of chipmunks who forfeited their lives in the name of horticulture.

Life! We've been long together,
Through pleasant and through stormy weather;
'Tis hard to part when friends are dear,
Perhaps 'twill cost a sigh, a tear;
Then steal away, give little warning;
Choose thine own time;
Say not 'good night', but in some brighter clime
Bid me good morning.

Anna Laetitia Barbauld
(1743-1824)

William Wordsworth said of this poem:

I am not in the habit of grudging people their good things, but I
wish I had written those lines.

*Alas, Wordsworth and his friends subsequently turned against her.
Mrs Barbauld is forgotten now, but in her day she was a figure to
be reckoned with. Beautiful in her youth, she had many admirers
– including, rather surprisingly, the revolutionary Jean-Paul Marat,
who in the 1770s was teaching French at Warrington Academy,
where her father was also on the staff. She later married Rochemont
Barbauld, grandson of a French Huguenot. According to her niece,
Lucy Aikin,*

her attachment to Mr Barbauld was the illusion of a romantic fancy
– not of a tender heart. Had her true affections been early called
forth by a more genial home atmosphere, she would never have
allowed herself to be caught by crazy demonstrations of amorous
rapture, set off with theatrical French manners, or have conceived
of such exaggerated passion as a safe foundation on which to raise
the sober structure of domestic happiness. My father ascribed

that ill-starred union in great part to the baleful influence of the *Nouvelle Héloise* . . . [She] was informed by a true friend that he had experienced one attack of insanity, and was urged to break off the engagement on that account. – 'Then,' answered she, 'if I were now to disappoint him, he would certainly go mad.' To this there could be no reply; and with a kind of desperate generosity she rushed upon her melancholy destiny.

Melancholy it was, for Barbauld grew steadily worse. One day at dinner he seized a knife and chased his wife round the table; she escaped by jumping out of the window. But she refused to leave him, and when he drowned himself in 1808 she was inconsolable.

The ancient Greek city of Aphrodisias in Anatolia is for my money the most magical classical site to be found anywhere. It is also the most rewarding, owing to the astonishing quantity of superb sculpture which is unearthed every season. In 2007 it yielded up a circular grave altar, with a clearly legible inscription. My friend Bert Smith, who is Lincoln Professor of Archaeology at Oxford and who directs the excavations, has translated it.

The stone sings of Epikrates's son,
Epikrates, who lies beneath this mound,
Still a youth. Now the dust [of the gymnasium] is left behind,
As well as the lyre he strummed and the Homeric songs
And the spears, and the round shield of willow with the fine grip
And the horse bridles now covered with cobwebs
And the bows and the javelins. Outstanding in all these things,
To Hades the fair-famed youth has gone.

Hades was, of course, nothing to do with Hell – simply the place of the departed spirits.

Entries from the Parish Register of Seasalter, Kent:

1734 Edward Trice and Mary Acros married at the Cathedral of Seasalter. A Bowl of Punch was made almost as big as the Caspian.

1734 John Powney Huntsman to that antient Corporation of crucketsoles the City of Canterbury and Miss Eliz. Johnson, daughter to the Devil's Own, commonly called a Bailiff, were married at the Cathedral of Seasalter.

1742 Buried John Ellis, a very strong young fellow and a great smuggler.

1744 John Housden, widower, a young gape-mouth, lazy fellow, and Hannah Matthews, an old toothless wriggling Hagg, both of Faversham, were trammel by Licence at the Cathedral of Seasalter.

1750 William Parnel and Mary Steed, a dolefull forbidding saturnine damsel, married.

My friend Brian Porter, who sent me these extracts, tells me that they were written by the Rev. Thomas Patten, who was appointed Vicar of Seasalter and Perpetual Curate of Whitstable in 1711, and held the two livings until his death in 1764 at the age of eighty.

'A product of Pembroke College, Oxford, from the start he was a law unto himself, and stories of his eccentricity have entered the local folklore. He not only openly kept a mistress, but drove to church in a butcher's cart, wore ragged, dirty clothes, signed himself 'Bishop of Whitstable', refused to read the Athanasian Creed, and would suddenly break off a sermon if he thought that any of the congregation would join him in a visit to the nearby pub.'

(Brian has now sent me further information on Patten:

In Archbishop Secker's visitation of the parishes in 1759, Patten is described as 'half-mad, impudent, poor'. When the archdeacon reproved him for not reading the Athanasian Creed, which the archbishop did, 'That may be,' answered Patten, 'perhaps he may believe it; I don't. He believes at the rate of £7,000 per annum; I at less than fifty.'

He died in October 1764 and was buried in Old Seasalter Church on the south side of the altar, his grave marked by a stone slab set in the chancel floor. Here it rested for over 160 years but in 1927 Seasalter received a new vicar, the Rev. Edward Thompson, a short, thick-set martinet with a stentorian voice, straight from the China Mission. Treating all and sundry like coolies, he had Patten's gravestone dug up and thrown out, saying he was not going to have so scandalous a man commemorated in his church. It languished among the weeds until the 1960s, when in that more tolerant decade (one which might have suited Patten) it was brought back into the church, where it now rests on a window sill.

The Parish Register with Patten's scurrilous entries is a treasured deposit in Canterbury Cathedral Library, sometimes on display.)

A letter to the Editor of The Observer *from Dame Edith Sitwell, 16 August 1961:*

Almost

Sir,

Only the fact that I am a Roman Catholic prevented me from committing immediate suicide on seeing in your issue of last Sunday that a person who writes as Mr John Wain does, disapproved of a poem of mine.

Edith Sitwell
W.C.2

As John Byrne – who sent me this gem – remarks, the Editor's heading is a masterstroke.

A letter in an Indian newspaper:

Dear Sir – During one of my recent outing with my family
at Ambajhani Garden, Nagpur, I was flabbergasted in seeing a
sizeable number of ladies, if my presumption proved accurate in
the age group of 25-45, including a good number of plumped ones
too taking pleasures in various merry-go-round item, swingers
('jhula'), slides ('slip') installed in the children park of Ambazhani
[sic] garden that are precisely meant for the tiny tots and hence
this deliberate childish act does not add up and taken as most
unbecoming of a responsible member of the society that projects a
very awkward scene to the onlookers which needs redressal.

The crudness with which these apparatus were being handled
one felt, some of this appliances would be annulled in no time.
Nothwithstanding intermittent intervention (with polite request)
from the dutiful sentry positioned at park, they remained
unperturbed from their contemptibly laughable activities.

However in the event one middle aged conscientous *[sic]*
onlooker who was keeping a weather eye open to the ongoing
whimsicality of the ladies in question, out of exasperation pointed
out one of the unabashed, dotaged lady, after briefing her lucidly
the basic purpose of installation of children's entertainment gadgets
in the park and the consequential affect there on due to over
tasking, urged her to vacate the swinger (jhula) in order to pave
way for eagerly awaiting children's merriment.

The unflinching lady instead of acting sensibly took his advice
as affronted and loosing her head she said 'what is so wrong in
having a little fun and that it is not so earth shattering or a heinous
crime that one need to be ashamed of.' The lady's voice echoed the
feelings of other like minded women who were also ludicrously
deriving volcanic energy by swaying the 'jhula' to and fro.

This have been an episode of one day. Presumably same recurred most of the other days too as people now-a-days swarming in Ambajhani Garden regularly in view of picnic season being already in air.

If memory serves me right, baring Ambajhani Garden and Baladdyan (Seminary Hills) Nagpur is not having a single impressive children park to take pride in.

The flora and lush green lawn of Ambajhani garden by all account have been a heart warming to the visitors. The jubilant children invariably have a mirthful time here, however, all their jocundness would perish in short order if afore mentioned vexed elements are not brought into account.

S. Ghosh
Aurangabad

Reflection on philosophers:

Nietzsche is pietzche
But Sartre is smartre.

Anon.

Dr Laura Schlesinger is, I am told, an American radio personality who dispenses advice to people who call in on her radio show. Recently she claimed that homosexuality was an abomination under Leviticus xviii, 22 and could not be condoned in any circumstances. This provoked an open letter:

Dear Dr Laura,

Thank you for doing so much to educate people regarding God's law. I have learnt a great deal from your show and I try to share that knowledge with as many people as I can. When someone tries to defend the homosexual lifestyle, for example, I simply remind him or her that Leviticus xviii, 22 clearly states it to be an abomination. End of debate. I so need some advice from you, however, regarding some of the specific laws and how to follow them.

a) When I burn a bull on the altar as a sacrifice, I know it creates a pleasing odor for the Lord (Lev. 1, 9). The problem is my neighbours. They claim that the odor is not pleasing to them. Should I smite them?

b) I would like to sell my daughter into slavery, as sanctioned in Exodus xxi, 7. In this day and age, what do you think would be a fair price for her?

c) Lev. xxv, 44 states that I may indeed possess slaves, both male and female, provided they are purchased from neighbouring nations. A friend of mine claims that this applies to Mexicans but not Canadians. Can you clarify? Why can't I own Canadians?

d) I have a neighbour who insists on working on the Sabbath. In Exodus xxxv, 2 it clearly states he should be put to death. Am I morally obliged to kill him myself?

e) A friend of mine feels that even though eating shellfish is an abomination (Lev. xi, 10) it is a lesser abomination than homosexuality. I don't agree. Can you settle this?

f) Lev. xxi, 20 states that I may not approach the altar of God if I have a defect in my sight. I have to admit that I wear reading glasses. Does my vision have to be 20 / 20, or is there some wiggle room here?

g) Most of my male friends get their hair trimmed, including the hair around their temples, even though this is expressly forbidden by Lev. xix, 27. How should they die?

h) I know from Lev. xi, 6-8 that touching the skin of a dead pig makes me unclean, but may I still play football if I wear gloves?

i) My uncle has a farm. He violates Lev. xix, 19 by planting two different crops in the same field, as does his wife by wearing garments made of two different kinds of thread (cotton/polyester blend). He also tends to curse and blaspheme a lot. Is it really necessary that we go to all the trouble of getting the whole town together to stone them (Lev. xxiv, 10-16)? Couldn't we just burn them to death as a private family affair, like we do with people who sleep with their in-laws (Lev. xx, 14)?

I know you have studied these things extensively so I am confident you can help. Thank you again for reminding us that God's word is eternal and unchanging.

A curious coincidence: some time ago my friend Martin Summers lent me his father's handwritten commonplace book, in which I found an acrostic sonnet which, the book informed me, was published in The Times *on the eve of the General Election of* 1931. *It was signed* 'D.C.', *and I am perfectly certain, from the style and circumstances, that it is by my father, Duff Cooper. Here it is:*

Steadfast of purpose have you proved – and true
Twice tied custodian of your country's fate,
And neither sought the many to placate
Nor feared the private malice of the few;
Lately, when civil turmoil fiercer grew,
Engendered out of misery by hate,
You were the statesman that preserved the State
Because the English people trusted you.
And when your work is ended, and the cheers
Loud echoing round you shall have died away
Down the long corridor of crowded years,
Welcome awaits you where you longed to stay –
In fields and lanes, in books and quiet spheres,
Not unremembered in your noisiest day.

I would earnestly warn you against trying to find out the reason for and explanation of everything . . . To try and find out the reason for everything is very dangerous and leads to nothing but disappointment and dissatisfaction, unsettling your mind and in the end making you miserable.

Queen Victoria,
in a letter to her granddaughter Princess Victoria of Hesse,
22 August 1883

Mr Michael John Wilkins at Tunbridge Wells Register, eldest son of Mr. and office on Saturday. Mrs. C.G. Wilkins of the bride wore a brown 36 The Chase, Tonbridge, man-woollen two-piece suit and ried. Miss Vivien Rosemary carried pink and white carnat Clark. Eldest daughter of M Tions. The best man was Mr. and Mrs. S.M. Clark of Mill Road Lobb. A reception was held cottages Claygate, Marden at 36 The Chase.

from The Hampshire Chronicle

A brass plaque near the south transept of Southwark Cathedral reads:

Susanna Barford departed this life the 20th of August 1652 aged
10 years 13 weekes, the nonsuch of the world for Piety and Vertue
in soe tender yeares.

And death and envye both must say twas fitt
Her memory should thus in brasse bee writt.
Here lyes interr'd within this bed of dust
A Virgin pure not stained by carnall lust;
Such grace the King of Kings bestow'd upon her
That now shee lives with Him a maid of honour.
Her stage was short, her thread was quickly spunn
Drawne out and cutt, gott Heaven, her worke was done.
This world to her was but a traged play;
She came and saw't, dislik't and passed away.

*'Traged' is a curious variant of 'tragic', and does not appear in the
O.E.D. Was the engraver nodding, perhaps?*

Simon Barnes is the Chief Sports Correspondent of The Times, *in which capacity he writes dazzlingly about tennis, the only sport that interests me. But I prefer his Wild Notebook – which appears every Saturday morning – because he can write like this:*

I saw no dormice. Very few people ever see dormice, even when there is a thriving population. Dormice are tinier than you would believe possible – you could hold a family in one cupped hand, if they would only stay still – they are nocturnal, they sleep seven months of the year, and they live mostly above our heads in the high branches of the hazels.

You might ask, then, what is the point of bringing them back. One answer is that even while living invisible lives, they are giving pleasure to humans. There is pleasure to be had in knowing that dormice are out there, living their busy, hungry, sleep-filled, furry lives; mothers leading a little funny train of babies through the canopy. There is pleasure, too, in being in a place where dormice are: knowing that somewhere above your head, dormice sleep and feed on insects and hazel nuts. The wood feels like a better place for the knowledge that there are dormice in it.

Jill Ritblat has kindly sent me this story from The Daily Telegraph *of 14 January 2004:*

Czech Composer who Plays that Funghi Music
by Kate Connolly in Prague

A Czech composer has produced a series of chart-topping symphonies and musical poems inspired by his passion for mushrooms.

Vaclav Halek, 66, who has been picking mushrooms since he was a child, has set to music almost every known mushroom growing in the region.

His latest compositions are compiled in a Musical Atlas of Mushrooms, a CD and accompanying book which is a hit with consumers in the run-up to Christmas.

Mr Halek, a gentle, rotund man, says he is happiest when wandering with a basket through the woods of Bohemia.

Taking a stroll this week through the marshlands of Klanovice, a forest on the eastern edge of Prague, Mr Halek focussed his sights on a flame-coloured bouquet of *flammulina velutipes,* or velvet shank, mushrooms blooming out of an elm stump. He put his mind to turning them to music.

Bending his head towards the mushroom cluster, he scratched his chin, took a deep breath and began excitedly to scribble notes.

'It's a spiritual moment for me', he said minutes later, his eyes full of tears, his paper covered in crotchets and treble clefs. 'I tune in to the mushroom, studying its shape, smell and colour and then I hear its individual music.'

Then he hums a nostalgic andante piece *Mushrooms for Cello* he was inspired to write before stooping to pick up the mushrooms.

Two elegant lyrical pieces for the pale yellow false chanterelle (for clarinet) and the winter trumpet (violin) follow before Mr Halek decides the cold has got the better of his arthritic limbs.

At home the composer, whose mushroom-inspired music has been used in Czech films, performs his work on a grand piano.

Mr Halek's hobby might find little resonance in countries like Britain where mushroom picking is not common.

But the Czech Republic's mushroom experts have hailed the compositions as an appropriate tribute to their passion, which has inspired some of the country's finest art, music and cuisine.

On 12 January 1993, The Village Voice *reported a comment by the Zambian tennis champion Lighton Ndefwayl after his defeat by his compatriot Musumba Bwayla in a recent match:*

> Musumba Bwayla is a stupid man and a hopeless player. He has a huge nose and is cross-eyed. Girls hate him. He beat me because my jockstrap was too tight and because when he serves he farts, and that made me lose my concentration, for which I am famous throughout Zambia.

The future Marquess Curzon of Kedleston (1859-1925), at the age of nine, wrote to his parents from school:

A hamper is undoubtedly requisite under the present circumstances. It must contain several pots of superior jam.

When he was thirty-five his style hadn't changed much. He wrote to his American fiancée, Mary Leiter, who was about to visit England after a year's absence:

Wide open and eager with delight will be the lover's arms into which (given a reasonable seclusion) you will spring, and already in anticipation are being formed the kisses that lips will leave on lips.

I remember Quentin Crewe telling me a story of Curzon at Hatfield. It was Sunday night, and he waved away the cold beef. The ensuing conversation went like this:

Lady Salisbury: Do you not care for some beef, Lord Curzon?

Curzon: I prefer to wait for the hot dish.

Lady Salisbury: I'm afraid there isn't one. On Sunday nights we like to give the servants the evening off and we just have cold meats. Do you not do that at Kedleston?

Curzon: No, Lady Salisbury. When I entertain, I entertain.

For we also wrestle with the Angel; and the man in whom the love of Eternity hath kindled will go lame in the things of time. For not without the anguish of the struggle shall the face of truth be seen; nor shall the day break without a benediction.

John of Salisbury
(1115-1176)

BONUS

From the Madison Institute Newsletter, Fall Issue, 1894:

Instruction and Advice for the Young Bride
on the Conduct and Procedure of
the Intimate and Personal Relationships of the
Marriage State
for the Greater Spiritual Sanctity
of this Blessed Sacrament and the Glory of God
by
Ruth Smythers, beloved wife of
the Reverend L.D. Smythers, Pastor
of the Arcadian Methodist Church of the
Eastern Regional Conference
Published in the year of our Lord
1894
Spiritual Guidance Press
New York City

To the sensitive young woman who has had the benefits of proper upbringing, the wedding day is, ironically, both the happiest and most terrifying day of her life. On the positive side, there is the wedding itself, in which the bride is the central attraction in a beautiful and inspiring ceremony, symbolizing her triumph in securing a male to provide for all her needs for the rest of her life. On the negative side, there is the wedding night, during which the bride must pay the piper, so to speak, by facing for the first time the terrible experience of sex.

At this point, dear reader, let me concede one shocking truth. Some young women actually anticipate the wedding night ordeal with curiosity and pleasure! Beware such an attitude! A selfish and sensual husband can easily take advantage of such a bride. One cardinal rule of marriage should never be forgotten: GIVE LITTLE, GIVE

SELDOM AND, ABOVE ALL, GIVE GRUDGINGLY. Otherwise what could have been a proper marriage could become an orgy of sexual lust.

On the other hand, the bride's terror need not be extreme. While sex is at best revolting and at worst rather painful, it has to be endured, and has been by women since the beginning of time, and is compensated for by the monogamous home and by the children produced through it.

It is useless, in most cases, for the bride to prevail upon the groom to forego the sexual initiation. While the ideal husband would be one who would approach his bride only at her request and only for the purpose of begetting offspring, such nobility and unselfishness cannot be expected from the average man.

Most men, if not denied, would demand sex almost every day. The wise bride will permit a maximum of two brief sexual experiences weekly during the first months of marriage. As time goes by she should make every effort to reduce this frequency.

Feigned illness, sleepiness and headache are among the wife's best friends in this matter. Arguments, nagging, scolding and bickering also prove very effective, if used in the late evening about an hour before the husband would normally commence his seduction.

Clever wives are forever on the alert for new and better methods of denying and discouraging the amorous overtures of the husband. A good wife should expect to have reduced sexual contacts to once a week by the end of the first year of marriage and to once a month by the end of the fifth year of marriage.

By their tenth anniversary many wives have managed to complete their child bearing and have achieved the ultimate goal of terminating all sexual contacts with the husband. By this time she can depend upon his love for the children and social pressures to hold the husband in the home.

Just as she should be ever alert to keep the quantity of sex as low as possible, the wise bride will pay equal attention to limiting the kind and degree of sexual contacts. Most men are by nature rather perverted and, if given half a chance, would engage in quite a variety of the most revolting practices. These practices include among others performing the normal act in abnormal positions; mouthing the female body; and offering their own vile bodies to be mouthed in turn.

Nudity, talking about sex, reading stories about sex, viewing photographs and drawings depicting or suggesting sex are the obnoxious habits the male is likely to acquire if permitted.

A wise bride will make it the goal never to allow her husband to see her unclothed body, and never allow him to display his unclothed body to her. Sex, when it cannot be prevented, should be practised only in total darkness. Many women have found it useful to have thick cotton nightgowns for themselves and pyjamas for their husbands. These should be donned in separate rooms. They need not be removed during the sex act. Thus, a minimum of flesh is exposed.

Once the bride has donned her gown and turned off all the lights, she should lie quietly upon the bed and await her groom. When he comes groping into the room she should make no sound to guide him in her direction, lest he take this as a sign of encouragement. She should let him grope in the dark. There is always the hope that he will stumble and incur some slight injury which she can use as an excuse to deny him sexual access.

When he finds her, the wife should lie as still as possible. Bodily motion on her part could be interpreted as sexual excitement by the optimistic husband.

If he attempts to kiss her on the lips she should turn her head slightly so that the kiss falls harmlessly on her cheek instead. If he attempts to kiss her hand, she should make a fist. If he lifts her gown and attempts to kiss her anyplace else she should quickly pull the gown back in place, spring from the bed, and announce that nature calls her to the toilet. This will generally dampen his desire to kiss in the forbidden territory.

If the husband attempts to seduce her with lascivious talk, the wise wife will suddenly remember some trivial non-sexual question to ask him. Once he answers she should keep the conversation going, no matter how frivolous it may seem at the time.

Eventually, the husband will learn that if he insists on having sexual contact, he must get on with it without amorous embellishment. The wise wife will allow him to pull the gown up no further than the waist, and only permit him to open the front of his pyjamas to thus make connection.

She will be absolutely silent or babble about her housework while he is huffing and puffing away. Above all, she will lie perfectly still and never under any circumstances grunt or groan while the act is in progress. As soon as the husband has completed the act, the wise wife will start nagging him about various minor tasks she wishes him to perform on the morrow. Many men obtain a major portion of their sexual satisfaction from the peaceful exhaustion immediately after the act is over. Thus the wife must ensure that there is no peace in this period for him to enjoy. Otherwise, he might be encouraged to soon try for more.

One heartening factor for which the wife can be grateful is the fact that her husband's home, school, church and social environment have been working together all through his life to instill in him a deep sense of guilt in regards to his sexual feelings, so that he comes to the marriage couch apologetically and filled with shame, already half cowed and subdued. The wise wife seizes upon this advantage and relentlessly pursues her goal first to limit, later to annihilate completely her husband's desire for sexual expression.

Copyright 1894 The Madison Institute

A
Christmas
Cracker

 2009

In what does the perennial melancholy of August consist? The sniff of autumn; the lengthening sunbeams; the tiredness of grasses; the persistence of convolvulus in the hedgerows; the disappearance from verges of blue geranium; few flowers, yet colour in the garden; bees bustling to accumulate whatever it is that they do accumulate before it is too late; and above all the quiet. This is the only windless month. Mornings and evenings are still. There is an echo in the firmament, for earth and sky become close, like the inside of a glass bell.

James Lees-Milne
Diary for 6 August 1983

THE BIG BANG

Brian Young sends me this reassuring little poem:

> Once in a saintly passion
>> I cried with desperate grief:
> 'Oh Lord, my heart is black with guile,
>> Of sinners I am chief.'
> Then stooped my guardian angel
>> And whispered from behind:
> 'Vanity, my little man,
>> You're nothing of the kind.'

James Thomson

(The 19th-century one, described in the Dictionary of National Biography *as 'poet and pessimist', whereas his more famous 18th-century namesake is merely 'poet'.)*

50% of Traffic Accidents Due to Women
By Mohammed al-Tweini

MADINA

A statistical study recently conducted has revealed that women are responsible for 50 percent of traffic accidents in the Kingdom because of sudden instructions they give to change direction, stop, or because of screaming and shouting.

Abdullah al-Olebi said his wife, who he picks up from school everyday, is a real headache for him because of her violent remarks about other cars and their drivers.

He said when she starts arguing with him, he loses his temper and this renders him much more likely to have an accident.

She said the reason behind her remarks is his overspeeding and added, 'Tough traffic penalties serve as a deterrent otherwise most families would have been sent to hospital'.

Fahad al-Marzouki said wives should be a factor of calm and security rather than a cause of tension.

Al-Marzouki's wife said the reason that she shouts at him is because he uses his mobile phone while driving and never inspects his car before he travels a long distance.

Jahr al-Dowsari said some mothers are directly responsible for many fatal accidents because they turn a blind eye to their sons' taking the car's keys without the knowledge of their fathers. By doing so, she mistakenly thinks she is helping her son to learn to drive so that he can help her go shopping.

Nabeel Abdul Malik said wives nagging their husbands to give them a lift or take them to friends is the direct cause of many accidents. 'Because they don't realize that their husbands need to rest when they come home from work. So, they drive in an agitated mood and this explains why they have traffic accidents.'

The Saudi Gazette
3 January 2007

It does not seem to have occurred to Mr al-Tweini or to any of the gentlemen he quotes that if women were allowed to drive in Saudi Arabia none of this would apply.

George Augustus Sala was perhaps the most popular and prolific journalist of Victorian England. In Things I have Seen and Places I have Known *he describes the dinner given to launch the new Cornhill Magazine in 1860:*

Anthony Trollope was very much to the fore, contradicting everybody, and occasionally going to sleep on sofas and chairs; or leaning against sideboards, and even somnolent while standing erect on the hearthrug. I never knew a man who could take so many spells of 'forty winks' at unexpected moments, and then turn up quite wakeful, alert and pugnacious, as the author of *Barchester Towers,* who had nothing of the bear but his skin, but whose ursine envelope was assuredly of the most grisly texture.

This letter speaks for itself. I am grateful to the author for allowing me to reproduce it here.

The Rt Hon David Miliband MP
Department of the Environment, Food and Rural Affairs
Nobel House, London SWIP 3JR

16 May 2007

Dear Secretary of State,
My friend, who is farming at the moment, recently received a cheque for £3,000 from the Rural Payments Agency for not rearing pigs. I would now like to join the 'not rearing pigs' business.

In your opinion, what is the best kind of farm not to rear pigs on, and which is the best breed of pigs not to rear? I want to be sure I approach this endeavour in keeping with all government policies, as dictated by the E.U. under the Common Agricultural Policy. I would prefer not to rear bacon pigs, but if this is not the type you want not rearing, I will just as gladly not rear porkers. Are there any advantages in not rearing rare breeds such as Saddlebacks or Gloucester Old Spots, or are there too many people already not rearing them?

As I see it, the hardest part of this programme will be keeping an accurate record of how many pigs I haven't reared. Are there any Government or Local Authority courses on this?

My friend is very satisfied with this business. He has been rearing pigs for forty years or so, and the best he has ever made on them was £1,422 in 1968. That is – until this year, when he received a cheque for not rearing any.

If I got £3,000 for not rearing 50 pigs, will I get £6,000 for not rearing 100? I plan to operate on a small scale at first, holding myself down to about 4,000 pigs not reared, which will mean about £240,000 for the first year. As I become more expert in not rearing pigs, I plan to be more ambitious, perhaps increasing to, say, 40,000 pigs not reared in my second year, for which I should expect about £2.4 million from your department. Incidentally, I wonder if I would be eligible to receive tradable carbon credits for all these pigs not producing harmful and polluting methane gases?

Another point: these pigs I plan not to rear will not eat 2,000 tonnes of cereals. I understand that you also pay farmers for not growing crops. Will I qualify for payments for not growing cereals not to feed the pigs I don't rear?

I am also considering the 'not milking cows' business, so please send any information you have on that too. Please could you also include the current DEFRA advice on set aside fields? Can this be done on an e-commerce basis with virtual fields (of which I seem to have several thousand hectares)?

In view of the above, you will realize that I will be totally unemployed, and will therefore qualify for unemployment benefits.

I shall of course be voting for your party in the next election.

Yours faithfully,
(Sgd.) Nigel Johnson-Hill

To Anthea, who may Command him Any Thing

Bid me to live, and I will live
   Thy Protestant to be:
Or bid me love, and I will give
   A loving heart to thee.

A heart as soft, a heart as kind,
   A heart as sound and free,
As in the whole world thou canst find,
   That heart I'll give to thee.

Bid that heart stay, and it will stay
   To honour thy decree;
Or bid it languish quite away,
   And 't shall do so for thee.

Bid me to weep, and I will weep,
   While I have eyes to see:
And having none, yet I will keep
   A heart to weep for thee.

Bid me despair, and I'll despair,
   Under that *Cypresse* tree:
Or bid me die, and I will dare
   E'en Death, to die for thee.

Thou art my life, my love, my heart,
   The very eyes of me:
And hast command of every part,
   To live and die for thee.

*There, it seems to me, is Robert Herrick at his best; but at his worst
– oh dear . . .*

   Fain would I kiss my Julia's dainty leg
   Which is as white and hairless as an egg.

And what about those lines from 'To His Saviour: The New Year's Gift'? *(The reader will surely not need to be reminded that New Year's Day is also the Feast of the Circumcision.)*

> That little pretty bleeding part
> Of foreskin send to me:
> And I'll return a bleeding heart
> For New-Year's gift to Thee.

My friend Bob Guthrie has sent me the following extracts from an American parish magazine, culled over a number of years:

Remember in prayer the many who are sick of our church and community.

The rosebud on the altar this morning is to announce the birth of David Alan Belzer, the sin of Rev. and Mrs Julius Belzer.

Tuesday at 4 p.m. there will be an ice cream social. All ladies giving milk will please come early.

Wednesday, the Ladies' Liturgy Society will meet. Mrs Jones will sing 'Put me in my Little Bed', accompanied by the Pastor.

Thursday at 5 p.m. there will be a meeting of the Little Mothers' Club. All wishing to become little mothers, please see the Minister in his study.

This being Easter Sunday, we will ask Mrs Lewis to come forward and lay an egg on the altar.

The service will close with 'Little Drops of Water'. One of the ladies will start quietly and the rest of the congregation will join in.

Next Sunday a special collection will be taken to defray the cost of the new carpet. All those wishing to do something on the new carpet will come forward and do so.

A bean supper will be held on Tuesday evening in the church hall. Music will follow.

The ladies of the church have cast off clothing of every kind and they may be seen in the church basement Friday.

At the evening service tonight, the sermon topic will be 'What is Hell?' Come early and listen to our choir practice.

Between 1968 and 1978 the number of obscene items seized by H.M. Customs and Excise was 5,870,368 whereas, during the same period, the number of prosecutions brought under the Theatres Act was just one – against a 1971 revue, presented in Manchester, called *Dee Jay*. It can be difficult to identify the harm in adult consensual sex unless another offence is also involved. J. Edgar Hoover, for example, once noted that 'the F.B.I. are powerless to act in cases of oral-genital intimacy, unless it has in some way obstructed interstate commerce'.

The Times, 3 *June 2003*

From Brush up your German *('Frische dein Deutsch auf') by J.B.C. Grundy, Head of Modern Languages Department, Shrewsbury School. Undated, but I assume the early 1930s. (I omit the German text on the opposite page.)*

In the Cabaret

The hotel porter whistles a taxi up. Herr and Frau Meyer get in.

Herr M. *[to the driver]*: To the 'Femina' Dance Club, please.

    [Within half an hour they are stepping into the dance 'palace'. Herr M. takes off his hat and evening-coat and gives them to a servant. Frau M. goes into the ladies' cloak-room, hastily dabs her face with her powder-puff, and rejoins her husband. The maître-d'hôtel installs them at a table by the edge of the dancing-floor.]

Frau M. *[looking round her]*: Ripping! Just look at those people doing the blues, Helmuth. We really must have some dancing lessons.

[The jazz band stops. The dancers clap and move off to their tables. The wine-waiter arrives and presents the wine-list; Herr Meyer, who feels full of joie-de-vivre, orders champagne.]

Frau M.: Helmuth, why do all the tables have large numbers on them?

Herr M.: That's because of the table-telephones. If you catch sight of a friend on the other side, you've only to turn this number-dial to get your connection.

Frau M.: Then I shall certainly ring up that fair-haired young man at table S; he dances divinely.

Herr M. *[not too pleased at the proposed escapade]*: Well, of all the cheek! In that case I shall send a pneumatic letter to that pretty little thing in the black dress.

Frau M.: A pneumatic letter? How do you do that?

Herr M.: Quite simple! You take one of the letter-forms, put it into a tube, write on that the number of the table you want it to go to, and send if off through the opening in the tabletop. The cartridge whizzes under pressure to the exchange, where it is sorted and forwarded.

Frau M.: Hush, look! Something's happening.

    [The lights go out. Spotlights are focused on the dance-floor,

which gradually rises to the level of the tables, so that a variety-turn may be presented. When it is over, the floor goes down. There is more dancing.]

Frau M. *[an hour later]*: That tango was jolly good! You don't dance half so badly as you think, Helmuth.

Herr M.: A little more champagne?

Frau M.: What are they up to now? Do you see how everyone is staring at the roof?

[Suddenly there falls from the roof a cascade of inflated rubber dolls: grotesque dogs, seductive water-nymphs, and so on. In a flash Herr M. becomes an unruly boy again, tussling with rivals who are also trying to catch hold of one of the floating rubber bathing-girls, and finally rushes back with his spoil to his excited partner.]

Frau M.: Top-hole! Congratulations, my dear!

[At 2.30 a.m. Herr and Frau M. and the bathing-girl drive happily homeward.]

How can one be sure
If true love will endure?
My thoughts this morning are
As tangled as my hair.

> The Lady Horikawa
> 12th century

From the obituary of Jonathan Routh – The Times, *6 June 2008:*

Jonathan Routh was a supreme practical joker and hoaxer whose star reached its zenith with *Candid Camera,* the hugely successful sixties television series in which unsuspecting members of the public were duped into making fools of themselves while filmed with a hidden camera, to the delight of viewers. It was one of the earliest examples of television voyeurism . . .

A tailor was persuaded to make a suit for a chimpanzee. Tourists were coerced into propping up a 'leaning' Nelson's Column. Once Routh dressed up as a tree, stood at a bus stop and asked: 'Does this bus go to Sherwood Forest?' On another occasion, he stuck his hand out of a coal hole and told passers-by that he was looking for Baker Street Underground station . . .

Routh once organized a 'silent recital' by 'an unknown Hungarian pianist' at the Wigmore Hall. 'Tomas Blod' performed '*Transmogrifications,* Opus 37, by Sandal' in which he sat at the piano and played not a note. Routh thought it 'a quiet success'.

On another occasion he posted himself from Sheepwash, Devon, to the offices of the *Daily Mail* in Fleet Street, claiming that he was too scared to go to London on his own. As 'livestock' parcels had to be accompanied at all times he was put in a postman's care for the duration of the journey and delivered for £2. The postman was silent throughout. Routh thought this episode demonstrated the height of English tolerance and good manners . . .

Finding himself at a loose end, Routh invented Jeremy Feeble, an 18th-century poet whom he contrived to get mentioned in the *Times Literary Supplement* and on the BBC Third Programme.

His first job was as showbusiness editor of the now defunct *Everybody's Magazine,* which published a piece he filed from India in 1951 while on location with Jean Renoir, who was filming *The River.* He wrote that shooting had to be suspended when the cast was struck down by 'dhoti rash, a violent infection contracted from low-caste washerwomen'.

This job was followed by a spell as 'Candid Mike' on Radio Luxembourg. In one broadcast he conducted a bizarre conversation with a London Transport inspector who had caught him travelling with a grand piano on the Underground.

The softly spoken Routh was an engaging, mischievous social anarchist with an acute sense of the absurd and an iron nerve. He eschewed money, preferring to barter with his paintings, especially for restaurant meals, and remained entirely unworldly . . .

On 30 May 2000, the Spanish Ambassador in London, Santiago de Tamaròn, gave a dinner in honour of Paddy Leigh Fermor. He suggested that I write a verse or two to sing after dinner, so I produced these two additional verses to Cole Porter's 'You're the Top':

> You're the top, you're the Oresteia,
> You're the top, you're Promethean fire,
> You're the sunshine on a Penteliconic frieze,
> You're a bowl of runny Hymettus honey – Euripides!
> You're the rise of the gates of Cnossus,
> You're the thighs of the Rhodes Colossus,
> You're the bubbling bard who finds it hard to stop –
> Which is why we murmur, Fermor, 'You're the top!'

> You're the head of the young Apollo,
> You're the thread we shall always follow,
> You're the million volts of the thunderbolts of Zeus,
> You're Leda's swan, you're the square upon the hypotenuse!
> You're the spume on the cliffs of Mani,
> You're the bloom on a frangipani,
> And you'll fill and thrill our hearts until we drop –
> 'Cos from Bath to Burma, Fermor, you're the top!

My friend Roy Dean, who has made several past appearances in the Crackers, thought it might be interesting to know how the original addressee of 'You're the Top' might have responded:

> You're the pits, you are Nature's error,
> You're the Blitz, you're the Reign of Terror,
> You're the nasty smell of a cheap hotel in Spain,
> You're the deep recession, you're repossession, you're crack cocaine;
> You're a creep, you're a pop star's worst work,
> You're the sheep in a Damien Hirst work,
> I am looked upon as the paragon of wits –
> But if, baby, I'm the cherry, you're the pits!

A few years ago there was a fashion for one-line jokes embroidered on cushions; but I was quite surprised, when visiting recently the house of Dr and Mrs Tan in Singapore, to see upon their sofa a cushion on which was inscribed:

Tolerability makes all the difference in inflammatory acne.

In September 1939, when Randolph Churchill was doing his annual training with the 4th Queen's Own Hussars, he was ordered to board H.M.S. Kelly (Lord Louis Mountbatten commanding) at Portsmouth and proceed to Cherbourg to bring the Duke and Duchess of Windsor back to England. Here is his account:

The First Lord [his father] had instructed me to wear boots and breeches and my sword. I knew that military officers should not wear spurs on board His Majesty's ships, but I thought they might be needed in the course of my mission and I had therefore brought them with me in my suitcase.

We arrived at Cherbourg in the morning. I had put on my spurs before going on shore, otherwise I would have been 'improperly dressed'. We were conducted to a large *salon* on the first floor of the naval headquarters, where we were received by what seemed to be at least seven or eight French admirals. The whole affair was conducted most ceremoniously. After a quarter of an hour the Duke and Duchess arrived by train from Paris. A *vin d'honneur* was served, and toasts were drunk to everyone and everything that seemed appropriate in September 1939. We then sat down, eleven or twelve of us, in large overstuffed armchairs in a large circle. I was almost immediately opposite the Duke of Windsor and perhaps at a distance of some eight or nine yards. Suddenly, with eagle eye and an accent of triumph, he interrupted the general buzz of stilted conversation. 'Randolph, you have got your spurs on upside down.' Bending my portly figure uneasily and uncomfortably over my Sam Browne belt, and knocking over with my sword a half-filled glass of champagne which I had put by my side on the floor, I found that the Duke was correct in his diagnosis of my military turn-out. I made abject and ineffective gestures of apology and exculpation: but it was no good. When royalty can discover a medal put on in the wrong order or any error in dress, it makes their day and they are not to be denied. This occasion was a gala day.

He strode across the floor and said: 'Let me put them right, Randolph.' Scarlet, expostulating and miserable, I rose and sought to deter him. 'Sit down, sit down,' he said, 'let me do it.' Obedience is said to be the highest form of politeness and down I sat, and there, in the presence of all the French admirals, scandalised and uncomprehending, the Duke of Windsor knelt down and spent three or four of the happiest moments of his life fussing and fiddling about with the straps by which my spurs were attached to my boots. I kept trying ineffectively to relieve him of his task; to no avail.

After what I suppose was only three or four minutes but seemed like several aeons of time, the spurs were adjusted to the satisfaction of His Royal Highness. Fortunately the tide proclaimed and compelled our departure and we went aboard H.M.S. *Kelly*. I at once removed the offending spurs in the forlorn hope that I should be twitted no more. It was not to be. The cup was not allowed to pass, and all the way through luncheon the Duke continued to tease me about my extraordinary solecism. I bore it with such good nature as I could muster, but eventually as he is a kind man he saw that I had received sufficient punishment. He turned upon Captain Lord Louis Mountbatten and said: 'Dickie, I know you are only a simple sailor man, but you have played a lot of polo in your time. You must have noticed that Randolph's spurs were on upside down. Why didn't you tell him?' 'Well, sir,' replied Lord Louis with that disingenuous charm which has served him so well in his various careers, 'of course I noticed it, but I didn't want to spoil your fun.'

Rebecca West on Henry James's The Golden Bowl:

A delicate creature swathed in relative clauses as an individual in shawls . . .

With sentences vast as the granite blocks of the pyramids and a scale that would have made a site for a capital, he set about constructing a story the size of a hen-house.

Over the past forty years, Henry James has made many an appearance in these Crackers – and I hope he will continue to do so. I have recently found a little gem, quoted by George Lyttelton in a letter to Rupert Hart-Davis of 28 February 1957. James had just heard that A.C. Benson was to write the life of Dante Gabriel Rossetti.

'No, no, no, it won't do. *Dear* Arthur, we know just what he can, so beautifully, do, but no, oh no, this is to have the story of a purple man written by a white, or, at the most, a pale green man.'

Two more that give lasting pleasure:

A trifle too punctually, though not yet quite lamentably, bald.

He spoke, as to cheek and chin, of the joy of the matutinal steel.

Anya Sainsbury has introduced me to Our Ballet, *by Alexander Pleshcheev, which contains this remarkable story:*

Marie Taglioni left Russia for the last time in March 1842, and the contents of her house were sold by auction. Among the goods was a pair of ballet shoes, which realised 200 roubles. These shoes were cooked, served with a special sauce and eaten at a dinner organised by a group of balletomanes.

My friend Peter Vansittart died on 4 October 2008. He was an eccentric writer, but one of a prodigious talent never properly appreciated. This passage comes from his marvellous book, In Memory of England:

Transformations dominated early imagination. People became animals, plants, gods; slave girls wed princes, rags changed to riches. Mystery religions taught transformation rituals as stages towards illumination, salvation, Paradise. The phenomenon was given pre-eminent literary status in Ovid's *Metamorphoses,* where girls change to trees or reeds, a boy to a hyacinth. In Albion lore, a traveller may find a cave and reach the Underworld; have his life changed utterly by answering a riddle at a crossroads, encountering a stranger at a ford, or entering an uncanny tower. A queen is bewitched into a butterfly, a girl into a swallow. Celtic art seethes with limbs foaming into branches, serpents, waves; twigs becoming foliage, sun-rays, twirling patterns. Ripples, writhings, spirals, tendrils, circles, mazes are endlessly interlinked, cut on to torques, weapons, cauldrons. This fluidity of line matches mental gyrations which, unstoppable, translate rites and events to myth, thence to legend, then history, or literature: Cunebelinus becomes 'Cymbeline'. Boudicca's torque, twisted and golden, mirrors the flowing intricacies of Celtic verse. Celtic and Northumbrian line, curls of fancy and life-cycles, make what Louis MacNeice called the living curve which is breathlessly the same, reflected in the multiple transformations of young Arthur in T.H. White's *The Once and Future King,* in the cyclic images of Yeats, the visual puns of Dylan Thomas. It flows through the convoluted fantasies of the Book of Kells, the webs of Gothic allusion, the elaborate traceries of English Decorated: the surge of the Baroque, with its flames, wings, sensations of flight, has parallels to it; it is there in Hogarth's serpentine 'Line of Beauty'; it creates sinuous figures in *art nouveau* and in the early twentieth-century Scottish poets styled the 'Immortals'. It mimes botanical growths, interweaves invention and repetition, the headlong and stylised, the erotic and witty, its convulsions at odds with classical formality, authority, clarity. Dark Age ornamentation was continuous celebration of existence, twisting and writhing, in all variousness, like larksong or the flight of swifts, from the days when bards, remembered as birdmen, wore feathered cloaks and chanted 'winged words', their song leaping skywards, their listeners rapt, enchanted, also feeling themselves birds, able to peer into heaven.

In Survival Tactics *he writes:*

Macaulay and Burckhardt had been excited by poetry to study history: and for me history was neither a task nor morality tale but poetry, sometimes clear, often muddied, leaving spaces where imagination could paddle, while speculating, amused or angry. Aimed at the future, at me personally, history was omnipresent, flamboyant as Henry VIII's codpiece, subtle as Charles II's face, strange as genius, elusive as a Jacobean ghost and still the detective story packed with secrets.

A letter from Lord Orford to the Norwich Bible Society, 1824:

Sir,

I am surprised and annoyed by the contents of your letter –
surprised, because my well-known character should have exempted
me from such an application; and annoyed, because it compels me
to have even this communication with you.

I have long been addicted to the gaming table; I have lately
taken to the turf; I fear I frequently blaspheme; but I have never
distributed religious tracts. All this was known to you and your
society, notwithstanding which you think me a fit person to be your
president. God forgive your hypocrisy.

I would rather live in the land of sinners than with such saints.

Orford.

From A Moment towards the End of the Play, *by Timothy West:*

I went on to be in a play of Hugh Whitemore's called *It's Ralph,* to be produced for the West End . . .

My chief memory of the play is of the opening night on our prior-to-London week at the Theatre Royal, Brighton. The play began with Connie Booth and myself arriving at our country cottage for the weekend, and letting ourselves in through the front door. This was in fact the only door to the set, and it was fitted with a practical Yale lock, to which I had a key. Unfortunately one of the resident stage crew, while doing something to the door shortly beforehand, had inadvertently pushed up the catch on the lock so that, try as I might, I couldn't get in.

What could we do? The audience could see me through the glass panel of the door, but that ceased to be interesting after a while. I turned for advice to Brian Kirk, the Stage Manager. 'I'll have to bring the curtain down', he decided, and went off to instruct the flyman. The flyman, however, having raised the curtain initially, had nothing else on his cue-sheet for the next fifty minutes, and was already next door in the Wheatsheaf. While Brian was fetching him, the very slim assistant stage manager, realising what was wrong, managed to squeeze through the gap between the proscenium and the edge of the set, crossed the stage and, smiling reassuringly at the audience, released the catch and retired again to the prompt corner. So I turned the key, opened the door and walked into the room.

It was at this moment that the flyman, having been hastily retrieved from the pub, brought the curtain down. Audience bemusement was now giving way to open laughter, and Brian announced that he was going in front of the curtain to make a speech. I was dubious about this, but bowed to his experience in these things, and Connie and I went back outside the door and waited while he sought his way through the central parting of the heavy velvet curtain.

When this was used at all, it was as a drop curtain, and probably nobody had attempted to use the gap in the middle for many years. Its murky folds were thick with dust and festooned with cobwebs, and when Brian finally battled his way through to confront the audience, the spectral pallor of his dinner jacket, face and hair caused actual alarm among the now unnerved patrons.

However, he managed to explain to them what had occurred; they gave him a round of applause, he fought his way back again and came offstage, and after a moment the curtain rose once more. I opened the door, and Connie and I walked in.

Whether it was delayed panic that made the Chief Electrician hit the black-out button at this point, or whether it was just the next logical step in the nightmare, I cannot tell; the timing, however, was impeccable. The stage, on which I had not yet been permitted to utter a word, was plunged into inky blackness; and our author, sitting at the back of the stalls and wishing that he were anywhere on earth other than where he was at this moment, got up to leave the theatre.

As he opened the door, the Exit sign fell on his head.

In The Times *of 28 June 2008 I read to my surprise that the first words ever spoken by Greta Garbo on film were addressed to a waiter, to whom she said:*

'Bring me a whisky, ginger ale on the side, and don't be stingy, baby.'

To which the waiter somewhat tetchily replied:

'What do you want me to do, bring it to you in a pail?'

(My friend David Scholey tells me that the film was 'Anna Christie'; the writer, Eugene O'Neill.)

In 1980 Peter Paul Rubens's 'Samson and Delilah' – splendid reproductions of which may be found instantly on the internet – was sold at Christie's, and bought by the National Gallery for $5m. Brian Sewell wrote:

With the auctioneer's premium, the nation has paid more than two and a half million pounds for a painting that, when all is said and done, is a picture of post-coital *tristesse*. Samson's is an unedifying story of harlots, arson, cruelty to animals, and random vengeance as vile as any atrocity committed by the IRA or the PLO, and he was as tiresome as Squirrel Nutkin with his endless riddle-me-ree. For the full squalor of the tale look up *Judges* xiv and read on.

Delilah was at least the third woman in his life: a Philistine, night after night she entertained him in her bedroom, seeking to entrap and betray him, and here he is, this hulking brute, who, after a last nuzzle at the proud nipples of her bared breasts, lies sprawling across her knees like a collapsed and sated Hercules, glistening with the exertion of the pelvic thrust, now snoring at the golden gate from which his battering ram has so recently been withdrawn. The idiot, after playing games of mild bondage with her, has at last told her of the link between his strength and his uncut hair, and she has called in the barber who, with faggot elegance of limp wrist and tiny tea-cup finger, goes snip-snip as the brawn diminishes to match the brain. Hairdressers have not changed in three thousand years . . .

This great sculptural block, conceived as a tinted bronze, is a monument to compassion. Her treachery is now irreversible, but Delilah's hand rests lovingly on the shoulder of this man who will never pleasure her again, and she gazes with dry-eyed sadness at the lush mouth and prickly beard that for the last time have traced their snail's path from nipple to neck and up the long line of shoulder to the lobe of her ear. The smile of triumph is reserved for the sunken mouth of the ugly shrivelled crone holding a candle for the barber, fixed upon his gelding shears, immediately behind Delilah, her head at the same angle and her profile identical, she makes the hideous point that with time the younger woman's beauty will collapse into toothlessness, wrinkles and the drab thinning of hair. Only at that age may a woman be gleeful at a brute's unmanning: for Delilah there is only regret.

Guy Wetmore Carryl was born in New York in 1873. He specialized in light verse, usually taking his subjects from Aesop's Fables, Mother Goose Rhymes or Grimm's Fairy Tales. He died on All Fools' Day 1904, apparently from an illness contracted while fighting a fire at his house a month earlier. He was thirty-one. Here is a fine example of his work:

The Raven

A raven sat upon a tree
   And not a word he spoke, for
His beak contained a piece of Brie
   Or maybe it was Roquefort.
     We'll make it any kind of cheese you please –
     At all events, it was a cheese.

Beneath the tree's umbrageous limb
   A hungry fox sat smiling;
He saw the raven watching him
   And spoke in words beguiling.
     'J'admire,' said he, 'ton beau plumage'
     (The which was simply persiflage).

Two things there are, no doubt you know,
   To which a fox is used;
A rooster that is bound to crow,
   A crow that's bound to roost;
     And whichsoever he espies
     He tells the most unblushing lies.

'Sweet fowl', he said, 'I understand
   You're more than merely natty;
I hear you sing to beat the band
   And Adelina Patti.
     Pray render, with your liquid tongue,
     A bit from *Götterdämmerung*.

This subtle speech was aimed to please
    The crow, and it succeeded.
He thought no bird in all the trees
    Could sing as well as he did.
        In flattery completely doused,
        He gave the Jewel Song from *Faust*.

But gravitation's law, of course,
    As Isaac Newton showed it,
Exerted on the cheese its force
    And elsewhere soon bestowed it.
        In fact there is no need to tell
        What happened, when to earth it fell.

I blush to add that when the bird
    Took in the situation,
He said one brief, emphatic word
    Unfit for publication.
        The fox was greatly startled, but
        He only sighed, and said 'Tut, tut'.

The moral is: a fox is bound
    To be a shameless sinner.
And also, when the cheese comes round,
    You know it's after dinner.
        But (what is only known to few)
        The fox is after dinner, too.

The most lavishly produced cookery book that I have ever seen is called simply Alinea, *the name of a new restaurant in Chicago which has recently taken fourth place in the San Pellegrino list of the world's best restaurants. The first five chapters are entitled* Toward Creativity, Experiencing Alinea, The Postmodern Pantry, Black Truffle Explosion *and* Where It Comes From. *The recipe for 'Wild Bass' begins – as all recipes should – with directions explaining how to cook it. Then we come to the question of how it should be presented, and I quote:*

Near lower right edge of square plate, lay 1 braised endive leaf, with tip pointed toward corner. Using small offset spatula, place line of minced braised radicchio perpendicular to endive. Toss lentils with large spoonful of sherry-walnut vinaigrette and season lightly with salt. Spoon 3 small piles lentils around endive. Top each pile with 1 smoked glazed walnut. Garnish with 2 mint tips and grind black pepper in small pile nearby. Near top right corner of plate, spoon medium spoonful of curried puffed rice. Place kefir custard square on top of rice. Garnish with 2 red ribbon sorrel leaves. Following diagonal of plate, starting at base of puffed rice and moving to lower left corner of plate, spoon large spoonful of mushroom stem dice and small mushroom caps. Place 1 beet envelope at end of mushroom line, near lower left corner. Garnish envelope with 3 basil buds and 3 basil flowers. Place blood orange half segment and small pinch of blood orange zest near center of mushroom line. Arrange 3 claytonia leaves and 1 nepitella sprig along line of mushrooms. Behind mushrooms, moving toward upper left corner of plate, place rutabaga ball, piece of pickled pearl onion, and medium spoonful of leek ribbons. Garnish rutabaga with small spoonful of braised mustard seeds and 1 or 2 pieces micro oregano. Top pearl onion with 1 juniper berry skin. Place 1 trumpet royale mushroom chip on top of leek ribbons. Garnish with 2 micro chive tips. Behind this line of garnish, in very upper left corner of plate, place 1 enoki mushroom cluster. Garnish with 3 leaves red mustard cress and 3 pieces micro sorrel. Streak small spoonful of red pepper pudding in diagonal line, following line of mushrooms. Place warmed, glazed bass near red pepper streak.

Speak, you who are older, for it is fitting that you should; but with
accurate knowledge, and so not interrupt the music.

Ecclesiasticus xxxii, 3

BONUS

In Perspectives in Biology and Medicine, *Vol. 32 (1989) pp.602-4, there is published a paper by Joan D. Levin entitled 'Homer Smith, Urine and Modern Warfare'. Smith, she explains, was 'not only the most brilliant renal physiologist of the century, but a distinguished novelist and historian as well. She continues:*

Though phosphate is important in the usefulness of urine as fertilizer, the nitrogen of its urea, ammonia and other compounds is of no less significance in this respect, and urine as a source of nitrogen supplies us with an heroic example of what man in his ingenuity, when hard pressed, can achieve. I refer to the sad plight of Selma, Alabama, during the Civil War. To prepare saltpetre for the manufacture of gunpowder, the Confederates had to resort to all sorts of devices such as leaching the earth from old smokehouses, barns, and caves, and making artificial beds of all kinds of nitrogenous refuse, having agents for this purpose in every town and city. The agent at Selma was particularly energetic and enthusiastic, and advertised in the newspaper as follows:

'The Ladies of Selma are respectfully requested to preserve the chamber lye collected about the premises for the purpose of making nitre. A barrel will be sent round daily to collect it.
John Harrolson
Agent, Nitre Mining Bureau

This came to the attention of a poet in the Confederate army, who responded lyrically as follows:

HE ADVERTISED FOR CHAMBER LYE

John Harrolson! John Harrolson! You are a wretched creature:
You've added to this bloody war and new and awful feature.

You'd have us think, while every man is bound to be a fighter
The ladies, bless the dears, should have to save their pee for nitre.

John Harrolson! John Harrolson! Where did you get the notion
To send your barrel round the town to gather up the lotion?
We thought the girls had work enough in making shirts and kissing,
But you have put the pretty dears to patriotic pissing.

John Harrolson! John Harrolson! Do pray invent a neater
And somewhat more modest mode of making your saltpetre;
For 'tis an awful idea, John, gunpowdery and cranky,
That when a lady lifts her shift she's killing off a Yankee.

This poem was printed on toilet paper and circulated all over the
Confederacy, and a copy was smuggled across the line to fall into the
hand of an anonymous Yankee poet, who replied:

John Harrolson! John Harrolson! We've read in song and story
How women's tears through all the years have moistened fields of
glory,
But never was it told before amid such scenes of slaughter
Your southern beauties dried their tears and went to making water.

No wonder that your boys are brave; who couldn't be a fighter
If every time he fired his gun he used his sweetheart's nitre?
And vice-versa, what would make a Yankee soldier sadder
Than dodging bullets fired from a pretty woman's bladder?

They say there was a subtle smell that lingered in the powder,
And as the smoke grew thicker and the din of battle louder,
That there was found to this compound one serious objection:
No soldier boy could sniff it without getting an erection.

*To these two poems Miss Levin has added a third, 'bringing this art
form up-to-date for the 1980s':*

Oh Homer Smith, dear Homer Smith, it makes a maiden blush

To think that national defence could turn upon a flush.
But that's enough of Civil War in ancient, dog-eared rhymes;
We need a new approach to meet the needs of modern times.

Our patriotic fast food joints might realise these hopes,
And spice their wares judiciously with radioisotopes:
The customers could eat their fill, and then each loyal feeder
Would soon become a urinary radioactive breeder!

And every little child, from San Diego up to Maine,
Would give to national defence what once went down the drain;
And even Ron and Nancy could give of what they got
And donate all the contents of the Presidential pot.

Forget about cocaine and hash, they'll fill us with ennui -
There'll soon be better uses for each worker's drop of pee.
And all those silly drug tests, they soon will be forgot -
No more of asking 'Are you high?' but rather 'Are you hot?'

Oh Homer Smith, dear Homer Smith, behold a modern sight,
The nation's urine harnessed for her military might.
And we can fry the birds on high, and fishes in the sea,
With fifty million megatons of radioactive pee!

ACKNOWLEDGEMENTS

I would like to thank all those who have sent me contributions for the last forty years of Christmas Crackers, but I am particularly indebted to the following for permission to quote extracts included in *The Big Bang*:

Watson, Little Ltd for D.J. Enright's *Paradise Illustrated*, 1978, published by The Hogarth Press; 'Practising History' reprinted by the permission of Russell & Volkening as agents for the author, copyright © 1964 by Barbara Tuchman; Artellus Ltd on behalf of the Burgess estate for Anthony Burgess's piece; The letter by Ogden Nash copyright © 1956 by Ogden Nash, reprinted by permission of Curtis Brown Ltd; Levin, Joan D. Homer Smith, 'Urine and Modern Warfare'. Perspectives in Biology & Medicine Vol. 32 1989, 602-604, © 1989 The University of Chicago, reprinted with permission of The Johns Hopkins University Press.

The Dovecote Press has made every reasonable attempt to trace copyright holders of material included in this book, but if any have inadvertently been overlooked we would be glad to hear from them.

INDEX

Nightingale, Florence, 250
Noel, Bridget, 246
Norton, Charles, 38
Norwich, Anne, Viscountess, 205
Norwich Bible Society, 342
Notestein, Wallace, 237

oak trees, 185
obituaries, 65, 135, 245, 264, 291,
    332
obscenity, 328
Observer, The (newspaper), 297
Odyssey, 147
O'Faolain, Nuala, 47
O'Neill, Eugene, 345
Orchestra of the Age of
    Enlightenment, 268
Orford, Horatio Walpole, 3rd Earl
    of, 342
Orissa, India, 84

Pakenham, Michael, 194
palindromes, 186
Palmerston, Henry John Temple, 3rd
    Viscount, 29
Pancatantra, The, 71
Paradise, 195
Parker, John, 147, 255
Parliament, 26
Parsons, Nicholas, 88
Patten, Rev. Thomas, 295-6
Pembroke, Reginald Herbert, 15th
    Earl of, 219
Pentecost, Dr, 113
Percy, Algernon, 250
Perowne, Edward, 192
Philip, John Birnie, 14
Phillips, Hubert, 186
phrase books (foreign), 123, 329
pig farming, 323
Pitter, Ruth, 87

playgrounds, 298-9
*Pleasant Mornings at the British
    Museum*, 116
Pleshcheev, Alexander, 339
poetry, bad, 203, 234
Polsky, Leon and Cynthia, 127
Porter, Brian, 53, 295
Porter, Cole, 334
Portland Group, 215
Postman's Park, London, 118
Pougy, Liane de, 119
Pound, Ezra, 64
Preston, Stuart, 101
Price, R.G.G., 55
Princeton, USS, 204
proofreaders, 134
Pyongyang Metro, 229

Quarterly Review, 36
Quickswood, Lord Hugh Cecil,
    Baron, 133

radios, 30
rail travel, 28, 217, 258
Raison, Simon, 230
Ralegh, Sir Walter, 181
Ranfurly, Hermione, Lady, 46
Ratcliffe, John, 89
Ravoon, Mrs, 198
Rayleigh, John Arthur Strutt, 5th
    Baron, 139
Read, Terence, 65
Reeves, John, 253-4
Reid Dick, Sir William *see* Dick, Sir
    William Reid
Renoir, Jean, 332
Repton, Humphry, 271
Richards, Sir James, 132
Riddell, John and Sarah, 82
Ritblat, Jill, 308
Roosevelt, Theodore, 154